The Versatile **Welsh Breeds**

Brenda Williams

For my Son,
Julian Bell-Mckenna

The Versatile
Welsh Breeds

Brenda Williams

yLolfa

First impression: 2001
© Copyright Brenda Williams and Y Lolfa Cyf., 2001

Cover design: Ceri Jones
Cover photos:
top: Broughton Roxanne, photo by John Britter Photography
bottom left: Synod Robert Black and Joan Thomas, photo by Hilary Cotter
bottom right: Maesmynach Midnight Flyer, photo by John Britter Photography

ISBN: 0 86243 577 3

Printed on acid free and partly recycled paper
and published and bound in Wales by:
Y Lolfa Cyf., Talybont, Ceredigion SY24 5AP
e-mail ylolfa@ylolfa.com
internet www.ylolfa.com
phone +44 (0)1970 832 304
fax 832 782
isdn 832 813

Contents

FOREWORD

It is always a joy to know that a book which deals with our Welsh Breeds is being published. Brenda Williams, in this book, has set out to cover many aspects of these wonderful animals including many from overseas. In particular, I like some of the showing tips which have been woven into her work. These will be of great help to the younger and newer enthusiast, whilst reminding the more experienced people not to be complacent.

This publication is a further illustration of the tremendous increase in popularity of our Welsh Breeds. For far too long the Welsh ponies and Cobs have been the best kept secret in the world, but not any more.

I.J.R. Lloyd
Derwen

INTRODUCTION

The four Sections of the Welsh Breeds should need no introduction as they are rapidly becoming better known all over the world. With their characteristics of good looks, stamina, boldness and brilliant movement, the breed has proved itself not only as a Riding and Hunting horse or pony, but also in Dressage, Show Jumping, Eventing and Driving, both in Great Britain and abroad.

The Welsh Breeds are our heritage and as such should be bred with the object of safeguarding the future of the breed. This can only be done by selective breeding, and putting quality before quantity. Over-breeding can not only cause a decline in the quality, but also in the market for our ponies.

In this book I have tried to write something interesting for the newcomers to the Welsh Breeds and to the showing game, and also, I hope, of interest to the established breeders both here and abroad.

Regarding the studs that are featured in the book, there is no favouritism as I requested information from many people. However, some of those who were invited to supply the relevant details failed to respond. Also, in some cases, I had insufficient space to include every detail or, indeed, every single stud from across the world who very kindly supplied me with their information. Hopefully, the studs that have not been included here will be included in a second book to promote our Welsh Breeds and Part-Breeds, as our performance horses and ponies of the future.

BRENDA WILLIAMS
CRUGYBAR STUD

ACKNOWLEDGEMENTS

My sincere thanks to Ifor Lloyd, Derwen, for his continued invaluable help and support, and also for writing the foreword to my book.

Special thanks to Meirion Davies and Richard Miller, Heniarth, who have both given me much encouragement, advice, and help in marketing the book. I would also like to thank Eric Davies, Maesmynach, for his encouragement and valuable help.

I also thank the many people who kindly took the trouble to send me profiles of their studs both here and abroad. I would also like to apologise to those who sent me information and are not included. Unfortunately it has not been possible to feature every stud in this book. Those not included should be featured in my next book, already in progress.

Many thanks to Bleddyn Pugh for so kindly supplying me with many of the photographs and to the other photographers who also willingly gave me their help.

Last but not least, a big thank you to my husband, John, for putting up with me when writing the book, and his help with the initial proof-reading.

CHAPTER ONE

THE WELSH BREEDS

When considering purchasing an all-round horse or pony you need look no further than the four Sections of the Welsh Breeds for, included within the Sections A, B, C and D, there will be found an animal of the ideal size and weight for any rider, young or old.

The Welsh breeds have been around for some considerable time. The Welsh Mountain Pony, Section A, was living in his original home in the hills and valleys of Wales before the Romans, and evidence of the existence of the Welsh Cob in the Middle Ages, and even earlier, can be found in medieval Welsh literature. An edict issued by Henry VII that all horses under 15 hands had to be destroyed did not eliminate the Welsh. Hiding in desolate areas where his persecutors failed to go, he continued to live and reproduce, preserving for mankind a distinctive strain of pony that today has generated enthusiasm among breeders and pony lovers alike the world over.

The Welsh Mountain Pony did not have an easy life in the hills and valleys. Winters were severe, vegetation was sparse and shelter in the main was an isolated valley, a lump of rock or a clump of bare trees. Yet the Welsh Mountain Pony not only managed to survive, but flourished. Roaming the hills, climbing mountains, running over the roughest terrain, mares and foals, led by proud stallions, were able to perpetuate the breed through only the most hardy of stock. Thus, through this environment, came the development of a pony with remarkable soundness of body, tremendous capabilities of endurance, and an extremely high degree of native intelligence. That the Welsh Mountain Pony carries a trace of Arabian blood seems beyond doubt. However they have maintained their own physical characteristics over the years. It has been demonstrated that the Welsh crosses well with other breeds and this is an important aspect of their versatility. There is a saying that the blood of the Welsh Mountain Pony of perfect type can improve on any other blood to which it is mixed, and this has been proved many times over.

The most famous Welsh Mountain Pony is *Dyoll Starlight*, and today the best Welsh Mountain Ponies and many of the leading Welsh Cobs still trace back to *Starlight*, *Starlight* being the fourth horse ever to be registered with the Welsh Pony and Cob Society (the first being *Billy Bala*), which was formed way back in 1901. On 16 May 1894, a small white mare named *Moonlight*, foaled in 1886 by a 12hh white pony, described by her owner as like a 'miniature Arab full of quality with a lovely head and a good shoulder', foaled a colt destined to become the best-known pony in the Welsh Stud Book, beginning the famous 'Starlight Strain' which was to have a far-reaching influence on the breeding of the Welsh Mountain Pony. The legendary *Dyoll Starlight* not only founded a dynasty of beautiful Welsh Mountain ponies, but was also responsible for the predominance of greys amongst the modern Section A stock. He was bred at the Glanrannell Park Stud, owned by Howard Meuric Lloyd. It is due to *Starlight* that we have the quality animal, free moving and with the especially beautiful head, which characterises today's Welsh Mountain Pony, and it was obviously through *Moonlight* that her son, *Starlight*, inherited the Arab characteristics that he undoubtedly possessed. As *Starlight* grew to maturity, it soon became apparent that here was a pony very much out of the ordinary. Mares were brought to him to form a stud and the prefix *'Dyoll'* was registered.

In addition to his phenomenal success as a sire, *Dyoll Starlight* was a big winner in the show ring. From 1898 to 1901 he won each year at the Royal Show. He was retired from showing but at the age of eighteen he was specially paraded at the Royal Welsh Show at Swansea and presented with a silver medal designed by Mr Lloyd for the Welsh Pony

and Cob Society. Back in the show ring again in 1913, he won at the National Pony Show, was second at the Royal, and the following year won at the Royal Lancashire and third at the Royal. When he was beaten as an old pony, it was by his sons and grandsons and so, for the next twenty years or more, *Starlight*'s descendants completely monopolised Welsh Mountain Pony classes.

The Welsh Mountain Pony, whose height should not exceed 12hh (122 cms), should have a spirited character, be pony-like and hardy. Any colour is permissible apart from piebald or skewbald, although an excessive amount of white is frowned upon, especially for stallions. The head should be small with a nice dished profile, clean-cut, well set on and tapering to the muzzle, with prominent and wide nostrils. The eyes should be large and bold, with plenty of width between them indicating a good temperament: the bigger the eye, the better. Wall, or silver eyes, are sometimes found and are frowned upon by a good many judges, so are undesirable, though not taboo. The ears should be small, pointed, well up on the head, and proportionately close. The jaws and throat should be clean and finely cut, with ample room at the angle of the jaw. The neck should be set square and true and should be long, thus giving a good length of rein for riding or driving. The wither should be moderately fine, a flat wither is of no use for holding a saddle or harness in place. A long forearm, well developed knee, short, flat bone below the knee, with pasterns of proportionate slope and length. Feet well shaped and round, and hoofs should be dense. Lustrous and abundant feather on the legs is most desirable.

The back and loins should be muscular, strong and well coupled. A good, deep girth with well sprung ribs is essential. The deeper through the heart, the better. The hindquarters should be lengthy and fine, not cobby, ragged or goose-rumped. The tail should be well set on and carried gaily. The hind legs should have large hocks, flat and clean with points prominent, to turn neither inwards nor outwards. The hock should be well set on a line from the point of the quarter to the fetlock joint.

The action of the Welsh Mountain Pony should be quick, free and straight from the shoulder, and well away in front. The hocks should be well flexed, with straight powerful leverage, and well under the body.

The Welsh Mountain Pony in the 21st century still reflects its early environment in terms of action, constitutional hardiness and conformation. The hardiness remains unaltered despite the passing of many centuries, but the conformation and the action have been improved and refined by human intervention and selective breeding policies.

The environment in which the Welsh Mountain Ponies lived was subject to the harshest climatic conditions. The terrain being extremely rough, with very steep inclines, strewn with boulders and shale, intersected with deep and fast flowing streams. On the upper ground there were many treacherous bogs and many areas were impassable. Vegetation in these areas was sparse and in the winter much of the ground was covered in snow. Living under these conditions the ponies developed as small animals and as such were able to compensate for the loss of body heat. They required less food in order to maintain a reasonable condition.

And so, to this day, the Welsh Breeds do better on a relatively restricted diet giving rise to the prime criterion of the Welsh Pony, which is that it should be able to survive and thrive even under these conditions. Thus today, it is highly unadvisable to keep Welsh Ponies on lush, rich pasture as they become grossly over fat and are highly susceptible to suffering from laminitis.

The Welsh Mountain Pony has mental characteristics to match his sound constitution and hardiness. He has a highly developed sense of self preservation, is shrewd and has an extreme intelligence that allows him to learn quickly. He is fast, courageous, sure footed, and he can be trusted, his kind nature making him the ideal child's pony for competing in Leading Rein, First Ridden and Cradle Stakes competitions. Also for adults he is a brilliant performer in harness.

The Welsh Mountain Pony has been described by many as being the most beautiful pony in the whole world, a fact which has remained uncontested. As a foundation stock for breeding bigger ponies and horses, the Welsh Mountain Pony is unsurpassed and in recent years the full potential of the use of Welsh blood in the production of modern riding competition horses and ponies has become much more widely sought after. Today there are Welsh Mountain Pony studs to be found all over the world.

The Welsh Pony, Section B of the stud book, height not exceeding 13.2hh (137cms), is the latest introduction to the stud book and not having been established as long as the other sections there is more variation in type. The general description of ponies in Section A of the Welsh Pony and Cob Society Stud Book is applicable to those in Section B, but with a greater emphasis being placed on riding pony qualities, with riding pony action, whilst still retaining the true Welsh Type of quality with substance. Having the temperament of their Welsh Mountain Pony forbears makes the Welsh Pony second to none in whatever field his young rider may choose. Today they hold their own among our top-class riding ponies both in the show ring and in performance competitions.

Early examples of Section B ponies were often a cross between small Cob stallions and Mountain mares. They were once called the 'shepherd's pony' as their job was to carry a grown man shepherding on the hills, and also they were more than capable of a day's hunting. In earlier days they were hardy and able to live out on the hills fending for themselves which the modern type of pony may not be capable of doing.

There is no doubt that the greatest influence in Section B breeding since the formation of the Stud Book was the famous Coed Coch Stud which, after *Dyoll Starlight*, exerted the same dominance over the Welsh Mountain through some memorable ponies. *Coed Coch Tan-yBwlch Berwyn* was one of the most successful of the *Coed Coch* stallions, having produced a whole generation of *Coed Coch* champions in both the Welsh Mountain Pony and the Welsh Pony.

Solway Master Bronze was also one of the most influential of the Section B stallions and combined the best blood of *Coed Coch* and *Criban* for he was by *Glyndwr* out of *Criban Biddy Bronze*. He retired in 1974 after siring over five hundred foals.

Another famous Section B stallion is *Downland Chevalier*, who was foaled in 1962 and is regarded as being the major factor in the modern Welsh Pony of today. Although *Chevalier* grew to over height he still headed the sire ratings between 1973 and 1980.

The modern 'improved' Section B pony is most definitely a riding pony of quality, and, by virtue of its size and action, the Section B of well-proven jumping ability obviously has the edge on the Mountain Pony in terms of versatility and the wider use made of the breed by the older and bigger child. It has perfect riding action, with little trace of the characteristic knee action of the Mountain Pony and the Welsh Cobs. However, there are those who claim that the refinements bred into the Section B have been gained at the expense of the bone, substance and hardiness which is the very foundation of the Welsh Breeds.

For many years the Welsh Pony, Section B and Part-Bred Section B riding pony, has held its own as one of the top ridden show ponies and today, the Welsh Pony, Section B, is in demand in all four corners of the globe as a competition pony, and it also performs equally well in harness, in which it excels, as do all the four Sections of the Welsh Breeds.

The Welsh Pony of Cob Type, Section C, with a height limit of 13.2hh (137 cms), and the Welsh Cob, Section D, with no upper height limit, though the majority are around 14.2hh, come from all over Wales and have been renowned for centuries for their strength, quality, handsome appearance and spectacular movement. These are probably the most versatile of all the native breeds. Always superb trotters, they are fantastic animals, and like no other. The Welsh Pony of Cob Type, Section C, is a superb ride-and-drive animal, up to weight and ideal as a mount to bridge the gap for young people between the pony and the horse, the Welsh Cob, Section D, which some breeders produce around the 15–16hh size. Although at these sizes they can lose their typical Cob character and appearance.

The breed standard as laid down by the Welsh Pony and Cob Society is the same for both the Section C and the Section D, except for the height limit on the Section C. However, the Section C should be full of pony character, having a typical pony head, rather than the plainer head of the Section D which some breeders prefer to produce and some judges have a liking for. The basic overall shape for the Section C and the Section D is the same as for the Welsh Mountain Pony. Both sections should have a deep, strong body, big quarters with magnificent legs and feet and, above all, the breathtaking movement with the great leverage from the rear and the whole of the shoulder and the foreleg. The permissible colours are the same as for the Welsh Mountain Pony and Section B Welsh Pony. Any colour is acceptable except for piebald and skewbald. However, a grey Section D or Section C is not the most desirable of colours to produce, nor is one with too much white, either on the face or too high up on the legs, and splashes of white on the body area are definitely to be avoided at all costs.

Both the Section C and the Welsh Cob were influenced by Spanish horses which were much in evidence in Wales during the 12th century. The Section C, the Welsh Pony of Cob Type, was the result of crossing Welsh Mountain mares with the smaller Cobs of the day. In the Mountain Pony breeding areas, Section C Cobs inclined more to pony character, as, indeed, did the larger Cobs, whilst in Cardiganshire, the heartland of Cob breeding, and in Breconshire, Carmarthenshire and Pembrokeshire, the type was far stronger built.

In years gone by in Wales, Welsh Cobs were

Welsh Cob: *Tymor Pele* by *Crugybar Mabon Mai*.
Photo by Bleddyn Pugh

Two year-old Welsh Cob: *Ruska Mister Pearly King*,
Henk Van Dijk, Holland

Section C Stallion: *Nebo Bouncer*
Photo by Bleddyn Pugh

Welsh Cob Mare *Min-y-ffordd Maid Marion*

Welsh Cob stallion: *Derwen Replica*
Photo by Alan Raddon

Welsh Part-bred: *Gernant Surprise*

Welsh Mountain Pony filly: *Sunwillow Georgina*
Photo by Bleddyn Pugh

Welsh Cob stallion: *Gwynfaes Culwch*
Photo by Bleddyn Pugh

Section C mares at Menai Stud
Photo by Bleddyn Pugh

Welsh Mountain Pony stallion: *Zonneweide Hamid*, in Holland
Photo by Janneke de Rade

Welsh Mountain Pony stallion: *Gleinant Snaffles*
Photo by Pauline Lloyd

Welsh Mountain stallion: *Trefaes Guardsman*
Photo by Bleddyn Pugh

Welsh Mountain Pony: *Ekbackens Black Jolly,* Inger Becker, Sweden

Welsh Cob stallion: *Mabnescliffe Advisor*
Photo by Brenda Williams

used for every sort of farm and harness work and many, including the smaller Section Cs, were used for hunting on the hills by full grown men. They were also supplied in large numbers between the wars to the Army as draught horses and troopers for mounted infantry: there was also a huge trade in Cob with the big city bakeries and dairy companies. For the farmer, he had to be fleet of foot, a good jumper, a good swimmer and to be able to carry a substantial weight on his back. He also had to be capable of drawing loads of timber from the forests and doing the general work on the upland farms, long before the introduction of the heavier animals. Later on, but before the motor car, the Welsh Cob

was the quickest form of transport for the doctor or others who needed to get from here to there in the shortest possible time. Nowadays the Welsh Cob has come into his own as an unequalled all-rounder.

The Welsh Cob is strong enough to carry any weight, it is infinitely enduring, it has the courage of a Thoroughbred, it jumps carefully, is extraordinarily sure-footed, hence the lift of the knee to avoid stumbling on rough ground, and is extremely sensible. It is also sound and easily kept as it thrives on minimal rations: lush grazing and indulgent feed are a recipe for disaster for this breed as it is contrary to its natural metabolism.

As the basis for producing the competition horse

the Cob has no equal. Cross a Welsh Cob with a Thoroughbred – some breeders like to put a Thoroughbred stallion on a Cob mare, some breeders reverse this procedure and put a Cob stallion onto a Thoroughbred mare so as to preserve more of the Cob character – and you have a brilliant competition horse unequalled for Dressage, Show Jumping and Hunting. Crossing a second time to a Thoroughbred produces the best of the event horses, giving the offspring better scope and speed whilst retaining some of the common sense and much of the constitutional soundness of the Welsh.

For the average horse-loving family the Welsh Cobs most certainly fit the bill for something easy to manage and to keep. They meet the requirements of all age groups, have the warm-blooded and lovable pony nature, are active, kind, intelligent and willing. They have never been used to the easy life. Throughout the ages they have flourished and worked on small Welsh farms sharing in the not always ideal conditions that prevailed, and this was the sort of life that made them what they are. Aptly described as the best ride-and-drive animal in the world, the Welsh Cob has been bred through many centuries for his courage, tractability and powers of endurance. Because of their heritage the Welsh Breeds are not bothered by some of the extreme variations of climate encountered around the world.

Today's Welsh Cobs are amongst the most valuable of the British Equine heritage either as pure-bred or as the basis for the breeding of sound, tough and talented competition horses. Many Cobs have been exported from Great Britain and Welsh Breed Studs can now be found in most corners of the globe. Also, pure-bred Welsh Cobs and part-bred Cobs in Driving, Show Jumping, Riding and Dressage can be found showing extremely favourable results in shows worldwide. One famous Welsh Cob stallion, *Maesmynach Viking Warrior*, recently won the British Horse Foundation Award for the top British-bred Stallion, by annual progeny winnings, in the Show Jumping discipline. (See pages 97-99)

At the Royal Welsh Show held at Builth Wells in July of each year, the ring full of Welsh Cob stallions on the Wednesday afternoon is a sight not to be missed or ever forgotten.

Welsh Cob stallion: *Hewid Cardi*
Photo by Bleddyn Pugh

CHAPTER TWO
THE WELSH PART–BRED

Welsh Part-Bred horses and ponies have been competing successfully for some considerable time, but have barely received the recognition due to them for their capabilities.

Part-Bred Section B ponies were winning ridden show pony classes long before people actually realised they were the product of a Welsh pony usually crossed with a small thoroughbred. These ridden show ponies are, to my mind, some of the most beautiful ponies in the world. Admittedly they are not everyone's favourites, but to me there is nothing prettier than a Part-Bred Welsh show pony with it's pretty, perfectly matched jockey aboard showing themselves off around the ring at a show.

The role of the Welsh Cob as a part-bred performance horse has been even less well known and publicised over the years. But, as the demand for suitable horses in all areas of equestrianism increases, there are now a significant number of breeders choosing to produce horses through cross breeding with native breeds and in particular the Welsh Cob. The Welsh Part-Bred horse is one result of this practice and it is now universally recognised and regarded as an advantage to have a strain of Welsh Cob blood in a potential competition horse's pedigree.

The Welsh Part-Bred horse has a minimum of 25% registered pure Welsh blood; in America it has to be 50%, and the Welsh input can come from either the sire or the dam. They may also be the result of crossing two 25% Welsh animals or from any other combination which ensures the qualifying 25%. There is no maximum height limit but the minimum height limit is 14.2hh, and they can also be produced by breeding up from the smaller Welsh ponies and part-breds. These horses are eligible at any age for registration in the Welsh Pony and Cob Society's Part-Bred register.

Welsh Cobs have been crossed with many types and breeds of horses. These include Irish Draughts, Warmbloods, Cleveland Bays, and Arabs. However, the most popular cross is the Welsh Cob crossed with a thoroughbred, and Welsh Part-Bred horses are increasingly in evidence in every aspect of equestrian sport such as Dressage, Show Jumping, Driving, Eventing and also in the show ring. They look set to be the competition horse of the future as they have the movement and character to work in all spheres.

In Show Jumping there is *Mister Woppitt* (50%), an International Grade A, *April Sun* (25%), International Grade A, *Uptons LB* (25%), International Grade A and *Waysider* (50%), also International Grade A.

In Eventing, *Mayday* II (25%), Advanced, *Master Diligence* (25%), Advanced, *Redwood V* (50%), Advanced, and *Midnight Flyer* (50%), also Advanced.

In Dressage there is *Llanarth Neruda* (50%), Advanced, *Billycan* (50%), Advanced, *Heart of Gold* (50%), Advanced, and *Dwyfor Taurus* (50%), Advanced Medium.

Show horses include Supreme Champions Show Cob *Just William* (Copperfield PC; 50%) and Show Hunter *Meridian Park* (25%).

CHOOSING WELSH COBS FOR BREEDING

As selective breeding programmes using Welsh bloodlines become established, greater numbers of quality Welsh Part-Bred horses will become available. The cross is now beginning to attract the recognition it deserves for breeding versatile horses for competition, leisure, or showing.

When choosing Welsh Cobs for breeding Part-Bred competition horses there are certain points that you should consider. Breed for size, but keep to type in depth, action and quality. A good length of rein is essential in any riding horse, as is a good temperament. Movement is extremely important: the animal should have a strong hock action with the hind legs brought well forward underneath the animal, promoting and allowing freedom from the shoulder, without too much knee action. Competition horses need good, strong bone with clean, flat joints, and – very importantly – you should also breed for soundness and performance. Lastly, equal attention needs to be given to the selection of the non-Welsh parent.

The Welsh Part-Bred Horse Group, in association with the Welsh Pony and Cob Society, is addressing the task of promoting the breeding and registration of the Welsh Part-Bred horse as a ridden British Competition horse. To encourage the registration and permit easier identification of Welsh Part-Bred horses in the field of competition, the Welsh Part-Bred Horse Group has formulated a series of awards, the aim of which is to promote the Welsh Part-Bred Horse in **open** competition at all times as the competition horse of the future.

THE SHOWING AWARDS

Welsh Pony and Cob Society Special rosettes are awarded to the highest placed (i.e. prizewinning), registered Welsh Part-Bred horse in In-Hand Hunter, Hack, Cob, Riding horse, various competitions, Sport horse classes and an increasing number of specific Welsh Part-Bred classes.

THE COMPETITION AWARDS

These are prestigious series of awards specifically aimed at registered Welsh Part-Bred horses participating in ridden affiliated competitions, ie. British Dressage, BHTA competitions, Endurance Rides and BSJA Show Jumping. There are trophies and rosettes in all sections. New for the year 2000 were 'The Pioneer Awards', a series of trophies for the owners **and** breeders of the most promising young horse (seven years and under) competing in Dressage, Horse Trials and Show Jumping, culminating in 'The Premier Championship' and the award of the Breeders Challenge Trophy.

PROFILES OF PART-BRED STUDS
GERNANT WELSH PART-BREDS

Barbara Williams who owns the Gernant Stud in partnership with her father-in-law, Evan Williams, at Neuadd, Ciliau Aeron, Ceredigion, started breeding Welsh Part-Breds in 1989 encouraged by her father-in-law as she had bought by accident because she liked it, a four year-old unregistered Welsh Part-Bred gelding which she had owned for three years. He was 25% Welsh, out of a Welsh Part-Bred mare, and by the Thoroughbred sire, *Big Ivor*. Barbara had a lot of fun with this horse, showing him successfully at county level in small hunter classes, taking part in all riding club activities at local and national level and eventing him at pre-novice level; she found this horse to be incredibly athletic, sound and reliable. At that time her father-in-law already had at home a thirteen year-old Welsh Thoroughbred cross mare, *Gernant Lady*, which he had bred himself out of a Thoroughbred

mare which he had bought locally, and which had a Thoroughbred colt foal at foot. Finding this foal a handful and not a nice temperament, he decided to use a Welsh Cob stallion which stood at stud in the same village, *Ceredigion Tywysog*, who was a Royal Welsh winner, and owned by the Fronarth Stud, at Pennant.

When Barbara moved from Anglesey to Ciliau Aeron this mare had a foal at foot by a Section C stallion. She had proved difficult to breed from and had been allowed to run out with this stallion for two seasons before she held. The result was a roan gelding, *Gernant William X*, not big in stature at 14.2hh but who had everything – ability, guts and toughness – and which was sold as a four year-old to Mr Ifor Lloyd of the Derwen International Stud. A first trip to Llanybydder Horse Sale brought an unexpected chance for Barbara to view some stallions and she fell in love with the Thoroughbred grey stallion, *Bee Alive*. She went home and persuaded her father-in-law to send his mare to this stallion and, in 1989, after scanning, an injection to encourage her to come into season and a further injection after service, she foaled a chestnut colt, and a further seven foals in the following ten years.

The chestnut colt turned grey, grew to make 16.1hh, was gelded, and named *Gernant Grey Lad*, out of *Gernant Lady*, by *Bee Alive*. Barbara showed him as a three year-old in local and county shows and it was decided to sell him as there were now two more youngsters at home. Having taken advice

Welsh Mountain Pony: *Heniarth Yabadabadoo*
Photo by Richard Miller

Welsh Mountain Pony: *Zonneweide Hamid*
Photo by Janneke de Rade

Welsh Cob: *Crugybar Mabon Mai* as a foal
Photo by Brenda Williams

Welsh Mountain Pony: three year-old *Zonneweide Norelja*
Photo by Janneke de Rade

Welsh Part-Bred: *Ascot Lisa Marie*, Australia
Photo by Gary Jameson

Welsh Cob Stallion: *Geler Llewellyn*
Photo by Janneke de Rade

Welsh Mountain Pony mare: *Gleinant Cherry Blossom*

Welsh Mountain Pony in Sweden owner Inger Becker
Photo by Elisabeth Weden

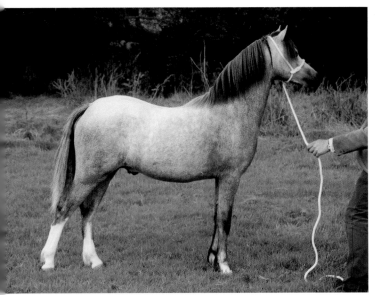

Welsh Mountain yearling colt: *Heniarth Mr. Milligan*
Photo by Richard Miller

Welsh Cob stallion, the late *Penllwynuchel Taran* in South Africa

Section B yearling colt: *Rhoson Shem*
Photo by Richard Miller

Welsh Cob stallion: *Fronarth Mab-y-Brenin*
Photo by Bleddyn Pugh

he was taken to the Malvern Autumn sales where he was the highest-priced three year-old, bought by Harvey Kaye, from Preston, England, who buys and sells show jumpers. However, instead of selling the horse on, he was retained by Harvey Kaye's daughter, Janet, re-named *Deep Dale Boy*, and the pair enjoyed a successful partnership. They were featured in *Horse and Hound* magazine in 1994, having just failed to qualify for the Wembley Newcomers Final, but they did qualify for the 1995 Horse and Hound Regional Foxhunter final. *Deep Dale Boy* was then sold to America and is a successful competitor abroad.

Gernant Lady produced another colt by the stallion, *Hipu Who*, *Gernant Castarn*. He also stood at 16.1hh and was sold to Yorkshire, where he competes in all Riding Club activities and also show jumps.

In 1993 *Gernant Lady* produced her first filly, by the TB x ID stallion and *Drayton*, named *Gernant Rosemarie*. A well-put-together filly, she was retained and was shown in both Young Hunter classes and Welsh Part-Bred classes. This filly has enjoyed a successful career to date, partnered by Barbara. As a yearling she won at Aberystwyth, was second at Pembroke, second at Anglesey and second at the Royal Welsh Show in both the Hunter sections and the Welsh Part-Bred sections. As a two year-old she again had a fairly successful season with mostly seconds at county level, and another second in the Welsh Part-Bred at the Royal Welsh. Next

she was shown as a broken four year-old and was first in the Hunter class at both Aberystwyth and Pembroke shows; also third out of eighteen forward in the ridden Welsh Part-Bred class at Pembroke, one of only two horses and fourteen ponies in the class.

Over the next two years she competed mostly in Affiliated Dressage. At age five she qualified for the Preliminary finals at Hough Hall in Worcester. She has gained 48 Dressage points and is now competing at Elementary level. During the year 2000 she returned to the show ring to compete in the ridden Welsh Part-Bred classes that have begun to appear in the showing calendar. In Aberystwyth she was first in the ridden section, first in the in-hand four year-old and over class, and Champion of the Welsh Part-Bred section. She was first in the ridden section, first in the In-Hand section, Champion of the Welsh Part-Bred section and Supreme Champion of the show at the Llanwnen Hunt Show. At Talsarn show she was first ridden Welsh Part-Bred and reserve Champion. At Ffos-y-ffin show she was first In-Hand Welsh Part-Bred and at the Welsh Performance show she gained first in the large Part-Bred Dressage and second large Welsh Part-Bred showing class. She is being aimed at both affiliated SJ and Pre-Novice Eventing for the future.

In 1994 *Gernant Lady* produced a liver chestnut filly, by *Drayton*, and at 15.2hh *Gernant Duplicate* is the smallest of *Lady*'s offspring. *Lady* herself stands at only 15.0hh. *Duplicate* was sold as a four year-old and is hunting with a family in Cornwall.

Lady produced *Gernant Atlanta*, by *Drayton* in 1996, a 16.0hh chestnut gelding. This young horse took a long time to mature but has a great future and is now owned by Colette Medland, the vet. He is being aimed at Eventing as he shows great technique over fences and has lovely paces.

Also in 1996 *Whose Lady*, out of a Thoroughbred by *Hipu Who* and by *Derwen Requiem*, produced *Gernant Surprise*, a 16.2hh dark bay gelding. This mare's first foal was shown initially as a two year-old and won every Welsh Part-Bred class he was entered in, culminating with Class winner at the Royal Welsh Show, and Large Part-Bred Champion. He was shown lightly as a three year-old, and then taken to the Malvern Sales in 1999 where he won the showing class and was the highest priced three year-old at the sale. He has gone to an eventing home and will be out competing as a five year-old.

In 1998 *Gernant Lady* produced a filly by *Drayton*, named *Gernant Abbey*. To mature at 16.1hh approximately, she is the first bay the mare has bred. Retained by the stud she will be shown as a three year-old and from there on be broken and hopefully take on a competitive career.

Gernant Lady produced another foal by *Drayton* in 1999, a colt, *Gernant Reflection*, again to mature around 16hh; the colt has been retained as *Lady* was then retired. He will be aimed at the show ring as a gelding when old enough.

In 2000, *Whose Lady* was covered once only by the Welsh Cob stallion, *Ceredigion Tywysog*, then twenty seven years of age, who was the obvious choice as he was the sire of the stud's original brood mare. The stud was hoping for a filly that could be used as a further brood mare; however, this was not to be and a lovely colt arrived instead. Unfortunately, not long after this colt was born, *Ceredigion Tywysog* died and the colt was named *Gernant the Last Prince*, as Tywysog is Welsh for Prince.

The Gernant Stud has a definite programme of breeding Welsh Part-Breds, firstly for the show ring as youngsters, but ultimately for the competitive arena. They prove to be tough, clever and have plenty of ability.

THE PENLANGANOL STUD

The Penlanganol Stud of Welsh Part-Breds was formed twenty five years ago by Jackie and Terry Jones, with *Penlanganol Swennie*. Her first foal by *Madeni Welsh Comet* stood 16hh and went Hunting, her second foal, *Penlanganol KC*, is by the thoroughbred stallion *Hustler* who was by *Sing Song*. KC's first foal went to Germany to show jump but unfortunately the stud lost contact with him and now the stud registers all their foals on the Welsh Part-Bred register and the British Horse Database. Jackie and Terry began to use Welsh Cobs because they are so tough and, crossed with the Thoroughbred, they are ideal for performing in any sphere be it Dressage, Eventing or Show Jumping as they are quick to learn and usually need to be told only once. An owner once quoted to Jackie that they are gentle giants with the brain of a pony. The Penlanganol horses range in height from 16hh to 17.3hh.

Penlanganol Jasper (Mister Woppit), International Grade A Showjumper
Dark Bay Gelding, 17.1hh
Sire: *Maesmynach Viking Warrior*
Dam: *Penlanganol KC*

Jasper has won just over £14,000 Show Jumping, firstly with Ian Wynne and later with Geoff Glazzard, with whom he has been for several years. He is owned by Mr John Palfree and Mrs Ingrid Christodoulou. *Jasper* was second to Nick Skelton in the Thomas Bates seven and eight year-old final at Wembley, where he was the Best British Bred horse in the whole series, winning his owners an extra £300. He has been competing on the Spanish Sunshine tour for several years and in 1999 went to Portugal. He qualified for Wembley in 1999, but his owners decided to withdraw him as he had had a very hard season being the main horse with Geoff Glazzard as both his top horses were sidelined. He has competed at the Royal Welsh Show for several years as his owners feel that it is his home ground, and has won several times there. He was the Premiere Champion in the Welsh Part-Bred Groups

Awards Scheme for three years running, 1995, '96, and '97, and is their Grade A Champion to the present day.

Penlanganol Vixen (Idle Debutante)
Bay Mare, 16.2hh
Sire: *Maesmynach Viking Warrior*
Dam: *Penlanganol KC*

Opal is owned by Mrs Nicki Court from Swansea, and has won £503 show jumping and considering how many shows she has been to this is very good. *Opal* has been the Welsh Part-Bred Group award scheme Grade C Champion for three years. Her owner has also won the Shoreham Bursary. *Opal* has competed at the Royal Show in the Working Hunter classes as well as the Royal Welsh Show. In 1999 it was a pleasure to see her and her brother in the show jumping classes on the same day, and both doing well. She is now in foal.

Penlanganol Chisum, (Mr Chisum)
Bay Gelding, 16.1hh
Sire: *Maesmynach Viking Warrior*
Dam: *Penlanganol KC*

Chisum is owned by Mrs Wendy Goodier, of Manchester. *Chisum* concentrates on Pure Dressage and is trained by Terry Downes FBHS. In his first year of competition he won the North Regional Final Championships and qualified for the British

National Championships at Stoneleigh, where he finished twelfth. In 1999 he finished fourth in the regionals and three went forward. He has now moved up and is concentrating on Elementary and Medium. Once again he finished fourth in the regionals in 2000, which was quite an achievement as there is a big step from Novice to Medium. He will contest this again in the future. *Chisum* won the Welsh Part-Bred Group Dressage champion and Reserve Premiere Champion in 2000.

Penlanganol Red Kite
Dark Bay Gelding, 17.3hh.
Sire: *Maesmynach Cymro Coch*
Dam: *Penlanganol KC*

Max, as he is known, is owned by Mrs Jo Gale, from Devon, and has been brought on very slowly as he has grown so big. He has £70 on his show jumping card from very few outings. He competed in the Burghley Young Event horse competition at Gatcombe in 1999 and went extremely well. He has also won both Working Hunter classes. He has entered and will be targeted at major shows as well as show jumping in the future. Mrs Gale was so impressed with *Max* that she has bought his full brother:

Penlanganol Assertive
Bay Gelding, 16hh

Sire: *Maesmynach Cymro Coch*
Dam: *Penlanganol KC*

Penlanganol horses are also Driving and doing Riding Club activities. Through her progeny *Penlanganol KC* won the British Horse Foundation Award for the Leading British Bred Mare (by annual progeny winnings) in Show Jumping discipline. And, as a result, Panlanganol Stud won the British Horse Foundation Award for her breeders. Jackie and Terry were presented with the award at the Hilton Hotel in London in January 2000 by the Chairman of the British Horse Foundation, Olympic Gold Medalist, Richard Meade.

WELSH PART-BREDS IN SOUTH AFRICA
Over the years the Welsh Part-Breds have been an outstanding advert in South Africa for the value of Welsh Pony blood. The ponies have excelled particularly in Showing and Dressage, while many have competed in Eventing, Show Jumping and Driving. Over the years many ponies from the Foresyte Stud of Ida Illingworth, and the Weydon Stud of Wendy Armitage, have dominated the Showing classes. Their ponies have proved to be the foundation stock for the most successful ponies in recent years.

The most successful show pony of the past years has been the dun mare, *Heatherlands Golden Girl*,

[*Foresyte Cambrian Golden Gorse, Foresyte Valiant Cymro* x *Belvoir Gazania* x *Willowsway Petroushka*], an Anglo Arab. This outstanding pony won every major Championship during the nineties.

Another outstanding pony was *Foresyte Bannut Heide*, [*Bannut Larkspur* x *Foresyte Chivitos Heidsich* x *Chvito* (Thb) x *Foresyte Valiant Bubbly*]. This beautiful bay mare was four times Breed Horse of the Year, In-Hand and twice Reserve Supreme Ridden Horse of the Year amongst her many successes. Her half sister, *Foresyte Fatal Attraction* [*Pendock Forsight* x *Foresyte Chivitos Heidsich*], has also excelled in the show ring. She has won the Breed Championship at the Welsh National Championships no less than three times and has also been the Supreme Ridden Champion three times at National Championships. She has also won consistently in Dressage at the highest level.

Welsh Part-Breds have excelled in Driving over the years. The most successful of these has been *D Leni Christmas Queen*. This chestnut mare has won consistently over the years in Private Drive classes and Obstacle classes. She has achieved, so far, eleven Legions of Merit.

Over the years many Part-Breds have jumped to Children's A Grade Level. The top Show Pony, *Foresyte Bannut Heide*, jumped to CA and also Evented at Intermediate Level. The imported Section B stallion, *Bannut Larkspur*, has produced a number of successful jumping ponies. These include

D Leni Bannut Ormany, Thb mare [*D Leni Bannut Nic Nacs*, x *Foresyte Kerrids Ballerina*], and *Bryndon Welsh Melody*, ex Thb mare.

Dressage has gained in popularity over recent years and Welsh Part-Breds are making a name for themselves here. The SA Children's Championship has been dominated by Part-Breds. In recent years *Bukkenburg Glips*, by a Section C stallion, and *D Leni Bally Boy* [*Foresyte Valiant Prince Llewelyn* x *Foresyte Kerrids Ballerina*], have excelled. The roan mare *Waterside Nile Beauty* [*Foresyte Bannut Glyndwr*, x *Bannut Larksour* x *Foresyte Gwenelyn*, ex Thb mare] has performed consistently and excels in musical Kur Classes.

CHAPTER THREE
CONFORMATION AND PURCHASE

A horse or pony that has good basic framework and is well made will be a pleasure to look at, and that is what you should aim for when purchasing your show horse or pony. But there are also practical reasons for good conformation, in that a horse or pony with good conformation will be easier to school, be more comfortable to ride and will remain more sound. Whereas the animal with very bad faults will have more strain put onto his structure, will be less easy – if not impossible – to school up to standard, and possibly be most uncomfortable to ride.

The perfect horse or pony is a product of an owner's imagination and here I quote an elderly gentleman friend of mine, a well-known and respected Welsh Mountain Pony breeder. An acquaintance once told him, 'I've got the perfect pony!' To which my friend replied, 'Well then, if you have the perfect pony, if I were you I would have it stuffed for posterity because there will never be another one!' When judging, one can always find faults, but the judge has to weigh up the good and bad points and compare all the exhibits.

The 'perfect' horse or pony regrettably does not exist but there are three ingredients that a champion should have plenty of – in addition to good conformation: loads of quality, an exceptionally good temperament and that all important 'presence', for without presence you might just as well leave him at home. The horse or pony that has naturally balanced paces and is beautifully proportioned should, in theory, be easier to produce for the ring. However, one often sees a horse or pony with conformation faults going like a champion and winning prizes, and this is because he has presence and has been especially cleverly produced. Thus, production can be a crucial part of showing.

Watching as many show classes as possible and studying the exhibits will give you the experience to enable you to pick a winner and you should also have learned that even the winners have faults.

First impressions count for a great deal and when assessing a horse or pony's conformation as a potential show animal you should begin by looking carefully at the overall picture. Has the animal got presence? Are you compelled to notice him straightaway, and not for the wrong reasons? Is the overall picture balanced, with everything in proportion? If so, then look further. If not, then this one is not your potential exhibit.

If I like the overall picture then I look carefully at the face and head. For me the face should be pleasant with not too much white, and the white should be in the right place which is the middle of the face, not all over the place and certainly not covering the eyes; a small star is preferable to a large blaze, the ears should face forward, and the eyes should be large. The facial expression should be one of friendly intelligence and alertness. A good head is a must: one that is too large looks unattractive and common, and also weighs heavy on the hands when ridden, whereas a too small one could indicate a mean nature. However a clever producer should be able to improve on a head that is not quite as one would like it, and a bad head is preferable to bad limbs or feet, which cannot be covered up. The head should be small and neat, well shaped, straight or slightly concave but never with a Roman nose, the cheek bones should have clearly defined curves, the eye should be large and kind, never small and piggy, and the ears should be small and neat.

The neck should be long enough to give a good length of rein. A short neck on a riding horse or pony is of no use at all, and it should not be too thick, especially at the jowl as the animal cannot flex properly. The working hunter pony may have a slightly shorter and thicker neck than the show pony, which is fine as long as it is in proportion to the rest of the body.

Every horse or pony, whether for riding or simply for showing in hand, should have a good

front . A good shoulder which is flat and sloping up to an elegant and well-defined wither is a must. A riding pony should have a good, deep chest giving plenty of heart room and a good girth line. The line under the belly should always be deeper in front of the girth than behind. If you have a pony with a poor girth line you will never be able to prevent the saddle from slipping forward.

A good top line, the line from the poll to the tail, is an absolute must in a show pony: it is also essential in an in-hand exhibit. A good top line is something all showing people wish for as no one can alter basic faults in conformation, such as a low set tail. After the head, this is the next part of an animal that I look at and if the tail is not in the right place I straightaway reject it. A tail that is set too low is one of the worst faults an animal can have. Tail carriage is also important: a show pony should not clamp his tail down tight to his rear end and neither should he carry it too high like an Arab. Both are unsightly and will lose points.

A quality animal should have sound, strong limbs with all joints looking hard and bony, with no tendency to roundness or puffiness, and the knees should be flat and well defined, with a good surface area for muscles and ligaments. The cannon bones should be strong, short and flat, with cool, clear, strong tendons standing out like cords. Pasterns should be short and sloping, neither too long nor too straight with clean, hard, fetlocks. The feet should be open and well shaped, not narrow or boxy, with a well grown, whole and clean looking frog which is not shrivelled or smelly, with the horn of the hoof free from cracks and ridges. The ridges produced on the wall of the hoof by laminitis are distinguishable from grass rings as they are more irregular and tend to merge towards the heel.

The forelegs should look straight when viewed from the front. They should be neither splayed nor bowed and the chest should be wide. If the chest is too narrow, the horse or pony will be described as having 'both legs coming out of the same hole'. The elbows should be free and not set too close to the body, as this restricts the freedom of movement. An animal whose elbows are set too close is said to be 'tied in at the elbow'.

A horse or pony's hindquarters and hind legs are the engine room, so they should be strong and well made. Looking from the rear the quarters should look nicely rounded with a well-developed second thigh on a mature animal but one not quite so developed in a youngster. The hocks should follow a straight line, vertical to the ground and should neither turn inwards – "cow hocks" nor the reverse barred hocks which cause the horse or pony to go wide behind which is extremely unsightly.

Cannon bones should be short and strong, definitely not long and narrow, and viewed from the side they should be vertical. Over-long cannon bones are a sign of weakness and undesirable in any animal. The overall line of the hind leg should not be too straight as this will inhibit movement. It should not be too curved between hock and buttock either.

Horses and ponies are said to have so many inches of bone and the measurement for this is taken just below the knee. A very small measurement here means that the animal is 'tied in below the knee' and horses and ponies which are like this, and are very light of bone, usually have other conformation faults, the cause often being attributed to too much in-breeding.

Finally you should view the animal from the side at a walk and trot, watching to see if he moves lightly and freely across the ground, especially at the trot, and that he engages his hocks well underneath him, and that he moves freely and well from the shoulder, using his shoulder to push his forelegs out in a long, low movement. He should not go along with his head lowered so that he looks as if he is going into the ground, or trail his hocks, or lift his knees like a hackney. His carriage should be naturally balanced as it is far easier to produce a pony that is correct from the start than have to take time to improve his action, balance and carriage yourself, although this can be done.

It is possible to find horses and ponies with natural elevation and extension, meaning that he has the ability and the conformation to really engage his hocks and use his shoulders in order to fling out his forelegs in a long action, with just a slight moment of suspension before his hoof hits the ground. Two such ponies immediately come to mind, the Welsh

Mountain pony stallion, *Gwyn Rhosyn Geraint*, who simply floats over the ground naturally, but regrettably is not broken to ride, and the Section B youngster, *Ccrugybar Pukka Pucca*, who has 'floated' from a foal quite naturally. Extravagant action like this is a delight to watch and expert schooling can produce it to a certain degree but natural movement has the edge on movement produced by schooling. Extravagant action like this is of course marvellous in a show pony, but useless in a leading rein pony – the tiny jockey would be unable to remain on board – and it is not desirable in a working hunter pony.

FINDING A SUITABLE PONY

First of all you have to decide what age, size and type of horse or pony you are looking for and if you already have your jockey lined up, you will know precisely what your requirements are. If you have not got your jockey then you have a free choice of pony, but then you will have to search for the right jockey to fit the animal.

If you intend to buy a 'made' pony with a showing record, and this is this best choice if your jockey is a novice, the very best way to find one is by word of mouth. Spread the word around amongst your friends and acquaintances and you will very soon hear of something that is outgrown and waiting for a suitable home. The genuine outgrown pony is the best one to buy and these ponies usually come with a trial period whereby

you can make absolutely certain that the pony suits your child. If things do not work out then, no harm done, you can return the pony and be free to look for something more suitable.

If nothing materialises by word of mouth keep an eye out in *Horse and Hound* and in the local papers. Also, check out the catalogues when you go to a show. In some of the shows there are often exhibits which are marked for sale. If this is the case watch the animal carefully in the ring to see if it is what you are looking for before approaching the owners after the class. Never approach an owner before a class as that is a sure way to get the owners' backs up: they will have quite enough to do getting the pony and jockey ready to enter the ring. You can also try approaching the breeders in your area. If they are producing their own breeding under saddle then probably they will have something already 'made' for sale, and if you are looking for something to 'make' yourself, then the breeder is the obvious person to visit if you are not breeding your own or have nothing old enough ready to show of your own breeding.

Watch the classes at the shows and decide which breeding takes your eye and have a word with the owners after the class. If a particular breeding takes your eye and the owners are not the breeders, contact the breeders as they may have something similar for sale or may know of something they have sold on which has come up for re-sale. They may also be able to put you in touch with other breeders who are producing the type of pony you are looking for.

An invaluable book to own is the yearly journal from the Welsh Pony and Cob Society in which you will find plenty of breeders of all the Welsh sections advertising their studs. Depending on how far you are prepared to travel to find your horse or pony, check out the ones within visiting distance that breed the section or sections that you are looking for, bearing in mind that not all the Welsh breeders actually breed all four sections of the Stud Book. Another point to be considered is that not all breeders of the Welsh Pony, Section B, for example, breed the same type of Section B. Some will specialise in the stronger, working hunter pony type, the true-to-type Section B, whereas others will breed the finer, show pony type of Section B. A similar situation occurs within the Section Cs. Some studs breed Section Cs with plenty of pony character and pony-type heads whereas others breed small cobs which might not be the type you are looking for. Make appointments to visit the studs: most of the breeders of the Welsh Breeds are a friendly lot and they will be delighted to show off their stock and are always willing to help. Do please phone first to enquire when it would be convenient to call, as there is nothing worse than someone turning up out of the blue on a rainy day wanting to view everything around on four legs.

Failing all else, there are of course Horse sales, but one does need to be an expert in order to buy, and if you are considering purchasing at a sale I would advise you to choose one of the official sales of the Welsh Breeds which are held in May, September and October each year. Here you will find genuine stock, have plenty of chance to look over your prospective purchase, and also the opportunity to have the animal vetted before payment takes place. Also, there are some real bargains to be bought at these sales on occasions, although some of the top breeding does fetch really big money.

Remember, all the normal, every day rules of buying a pony also apply to a show pony. Ask about his manners: is he good in the stable, to groom, trim, clip and plait? Does he load easily? It is no use having a beautiful pony if you cannot get it into the lorry to go to a show. Does he travel well? Is he good in traffic? Think of all those lorries and trailers on the show ground! Find out as much about the pony from the seller as you can. His stable routine, his likes and dislikes, what food he is used to, how much exercise he has, and his previous show records, if any. And, very important, is he easy to catch when turned out?

You should never consider buying a horse or pony without having your vet give it a full examination. That way you know you are safe and the animal has no hidden faults or defects that you have not been able to spot for yourself. If your vet passes the pony be sure to have him measured even if the pony has a life height certificate. There have been cases where heights have been objected to and even if the pony is just a fraction over he could be 'measured out' at a later date, which means he could never compete in that particular height class again. Also, be sure to make certain that his registration papers are in order as these are very valuable to you especially if you decide, in the case of a mare, to breed from the pony at a later date.

In conclusion, it is essential that you buy the kind of pony that you like personally, and here I quote my elderly breeder friend again: 'The type of ponies that I breed, and keep, are the ones that give me pleasure to look at.' This, I think, is what keeping horses and ponies is all about.

Lastly, when purchasing a horse or pony the first rule should be to buy the very best you can afford. Scrimping on the purchase price means skimping on the quality and if your intentions are to show and/or, breed, quality should be your top priority. Having said this, personally I would be inclined not to buy at all unless I could afford the very best. Far better to be without until you can have a top class animal, as they all eat the same amount of food whether they have quality or not.

CHAPTER FOUR

BREEDING

Breeding horses and ponies can be an enjoyable, fascinating and rewarding business and breeding is the basis of the entire horse world. All foals are adorable when they are born, they are a miracle to behold and there is tremendous satisfaction to be had in producing a quality foal from your mare. However, to be successful, your reasons for going into breeding must be valid ones as it is expensive to breed horses and ponies, and unless the job is done correctly the breeder can easily incur a loss instead of a profit. One does hear of phenomenal prices being paid for foals on occasions, but as a breeder you will only be in a position to command high prices for your stock if you keep only quality mares, covering them with top quality stallions.

To begin with there is the service fee which can vary tremendously from stud to stud. For a Welsh Cob, Section D, this can vary between a hundred pounds and several hundred pounds and at some studs there can be the added burden of VAT on top. The fee for a Section C stallion can cost anything from sixty to a few hundred pounds, the Welsh pony, Section B, from around one hundred and upwards and the Welsh Mountain Pony from forty up to a couple of hundred pounds. In all four sections the price is dependent on the quality and breeding of the stallion, and the quality and performance of the stock which he has already produced. The more prizes his progeny have won, the higher his fee will be.

Added to the cost of the service fee, the cost of keeping the mare for eleven months should be considered, which of course will include the extra rations she will need to keep her healthy and in the condition she needs to be in to produce a healthy foal. On top of this there is the cost of keeping the mare and foal in tip top condition until the foal is ready for weaning, ideally when it is five months old. All this costs serious money but, having said this, at the end of the day you could have produced a foal worth a few thousands and end up with a healthy profit, although you must bear in mind that this is not always the case.

It has been said that you breed what God gives you, but you can buy what you want, and this is unfortunately very true. Breeding is always a gamble, the mating of two perfect specimens cannot be guaranteed to produce another perfect specimen but, even so, careful selection of breeding stock should always be paramount in the breeder's mind. We must therefore be careful with our breeding policies and study the pedigrees of the stallions and mares that we use, asking ourselves what we are trying to breed and for what purpose we are breeding them and, most importantly, are the type of stock you wish to breed going to be the type to safeguard the future of the Welsh Breeds? Do you also want to breed quality stock to enjoy yourself and for other people to enjoy? If so, these are good reasons to begin breeding your own stock and starting a stud.

The Welsh Breeds and Part-Bred Welsh are a sound stud business proposition being extremely popular and becoming increasingly more so each year as more and more people become aware of their versatility. Take for example, *Maesmynach Viking Warrior*, the Welsh Cob Section D stallion who broke new ground in 1997 when he won the British Horse Foundation Award for the top stallion born in 1985 or after by progeny winnings in show jumping. Standing at 15.3hh *Measmynach Viking Warrior* has the character and presence that the true, old Cardiganshire Welsh Cobs possess and has the strength, stamina and intelligence to produce top class performance horses. This horse also possesses a fantastically kind temperament as all the Maesmynach stallions do.

Versatility is the byword for the Welsh Breeds, which is a good enough reason in itself for deciding to breed them. All four Sections can of course be bred and shown in the In-Hand classes, thus giving those of us who no longer ride for various reasons, enjoyment in the show ring. In addition all four Sections are capable of excelling in the various disciplines of Ridden Showing, Dressage, Jumping, Eventing and Driving.

Having decided that your reasons for breeding the Welsh Breeds are valid ones, you then have to decide which Section or Sections you are interested in keeping. Personal preferences are naturally number one priority, but other important considerations are your personal circumstances, and your facilities. For instance, if your family consists of tiny children, then Welsh Mountain ponies and Section B ponies would be the more suitable choice; also, as your family grows, you can follow through the Sections with them. However, if you do not have a family and are not likely to have one, then your choice is an open one and you will then have to find suitable jockeys to ride your produce for you.

Once you have decided on your favourite Sections you then have to think about which type of animal you wish to breed within those Sections. If you have chosen Welsh Cobs, do you want to breed animals around 14.2hh, or do you prefer the larger 15hh–15.2hh cobs, and are you intending to produce breeding or riding stock? Do you want to breed the good old-fashioned type of Section B with plenty of bone as breeding stock, or do you prefer the lighter, finer-boned type suitable for

Riding Pony classes? The same applies to the Section As. The Section Cs are either the type with 'pony character' or the type that resembles a small cob, with the cobbier type of head. The choice is up to you.

Choose your foundation stock with great care as these will determine the quality of the offspring you produce. When considering purchasing a mare for breeding, it is best to choose one who has proven herself by producing the quality of stock that you wish to breed yourself. Breeding soundness and conformation are important, and also a good reproductive history, and if you can see some of her offspring this will help you in deciding if she has the qualities that you need. A good temperament is essential. Your foal will be with its mother for some months and will be very much influenced by her behaviour and temperament. Cross and aggressive mares often rear like-minded foals. Mares that are difficult to catch also teach their foals to avoid humans. The ideal brood mare should like people, be tolerant of being handled, be social with other horses, and be viceless and willing. Ideally you might find a brood mare going under saddle, which is a good test of temperament.

The age of the mare is not of vital importance provided she is not too old, as long as she is in good health, and has previously bred foals. However, foaling is easier on younger mares, but be careful, breeding at too early an age can take away from the normal growth and development of the younger mare. It is best to wait until a mare is at least three years of age before covering her, so she has her first foal after reaching the age of four.

The brood mare should be free from hereditary faults and unsoundness, including any defects in either the jaws or teeth. Good basic bone structure and soundness, conformation, and a healthy genetic background are also important. To perpetuate any faults is not only unwise but pointless, the standard should surely improve, rather than deteriorate and indiscriminate breeding can only produce inferior stock which brings the breed into disrepute. A brood mare needs to be roomy, with sufficient width at the pelvis for foaling to be trouble free, she should also have a good barrel with plenty of length from hip to hock.

When buying a mare take your time, do not rush into anything, make absolutely certain that the animal suits your criteria before you finally decide to purchase. Hopefully she will be with you for a long time so you cannot afford to make mistakes by making hasty decisions. Before you begin looking you should have a very good idea of the breeding you like, in which case phone the stud and make an appointment to see their stock. Most stud owners of the Welsh Breeds are delighted to show off their stock of which they are justifiably proud, but please do them the courtesy of making an appointment first. They are busy people, particularly in the spring and early summer. And just turning up on their yard when the whim takes you is not always a good idea. It is common sense to view as many prospective 'purchases' as possible before deciding on which one is the right one for you, so visit as many studs as you can within your immediate area. You will then know exactly what is available for sale at that time, and also the prices being asked for the animals. Do not be misled into thinking that the most expensive is necessarily the best: of course it can be, but it does not always follow that it is. Obviously an animal with a show record will cost a great deal more than one which has not been shown at all, and will, presumably, win you lots of prizes should you wish to show yourself, but an unshown animal can be a lot of fun, especially when you start winning the rosettes with it from scratch.

Another place to find stock for sale is at the official breed sales for the Welsh Breeds, the Fayre Oaks sale in September is the one for the Welsh Mountain ponies, Sections Bs, Part-breds and geldings, and on the Royal Welsh Showground, at Builth Wells in May and October of each year. The May sale is a one-day sale covering all the four Sections, Part-Breds and geldings. The October sale, which covers Welsh Cobs and Welsh Ponies of Cob Type, foals, youngstock, Part-Breds and geldings, is held on the Friday, Saturday and Monday. If you are considering buying at any of these sales, catalogues can be bought well in advance from the Auctioneers. Study them carefully and if something takes your fancy you may be able to make an appointment to view the animal at home prior to the sale, which can be extremely useful.

When choosing a stallion, apart from looking at ways in which he will compensate for the mare's weaker areas, always look towards upgrading the mare as standards are improving all the time. It is commonsense not to use a stallion with weak hindlegs if this is not your mare's strongest point, or use a stallion that is light of bone and lacks scope and substance if your mare is of the same build. Strong features in the stallion should counter any shortcomings on the mare's part. To produce a good quality foal you will need a good quality mare to put to a good quality stallion. Before viewing stallions be critical about your mare, sizing up her faults and weaknesses if she has any, and only when you have done this should you start looking through the stud books to see which stallions you think might suit your mare.

If possible it is better to choose a mature stallion who has proved himself and has plenty of offspring which you can look at, and make a decision based on them. It does not necessarily matter what a stallion looks like himself; it is what he produces that counts, although a good-looking stallion is preferable. It is the stallion which is consistently producing quality foals which are good in colour, not having too much white, or worse still, too much white in undesirable places, have good bone and movement which is extremely important when breeding the Welsh Breeds. Also the one who has a good temperament is the one to choose providing he will suit your mare.

Then there are several other points to consider. Is the breed going to enhance the progeny in type and bone? Does the stallion have points in his conformation that will better your mare's? For instance, if your mare tends to be long in the back, is the stallion compact enough to compensate? Does the stallion differ greatly in size from the height and build of your mare? Does the stallion show presence, a very important trait for offspring?

You also need to check what colour the stallion is known to predominantly throw in his offspring. Does he always throw a lot of white, or does he never throw white? This is a very important point because in the Welsh Cobs and the Welsh Pony of Cob Type especially, a medium amount of white on an animal is much sought after. An animal with a small star or neat blaze and four even white socks is greatly prized amongst breeders. Whereas an animal with too much white on the face and legs can sometimes look horrendous, especially if it has a blaze covering most of its face and extending to the sides of the head. White patches on the body are most definitely frowned upon, whilst silver eyes are not much liked amongst breeders and many judges. Last but far from least, do you personally like the stallion? At the end of the day has he got enough presence to appeal to you? He must catch your eye.

Breeding quality is never guaranteed whatever stallion you use on your mares, but it is hoped that the stallion you choose will improve the points of

your mare that are weak, and that his bloodlines are strong so that he will 'stamp' his stock. It is known that a mare normally gives a minimum of fifty per cent of her own genes to her offspring, and it could be as much as eighty per cent, thus the mares line is most important in all pedigrees for that reason. Stallions and mares must complement one another. The breeder must keep in mind that the mare is capable of limiting the quality of her foal, regardless of the quality of its sire. You must also keep in mind that breeding is always a gamble: you may think you have everything right and you are bound to have a beautiful foal – sometimes you do and sometimes you do not. The same partnership of mare and stallion can produce a quality foal over and over again and then, for no apparent reason, a foal arrives which is nowhere near as good as its brothers and sisters. At the end of the day you get what you get, it is that simple!

If you like the stallion and are completely satisfied with what you see around you then the next question is the stud fee. If this is within your price range do ask whether or not there is VAT payable on top, especially if you are not yet in a position to claim this back: it could add quite a hefty sum onto the price. You also need to check the position if your mare turns out not to be in foal when the time comes, is there a 'no foal, fee return' available? You will no doubt wish to return the mare to the stallion the following year if she is unfortunate not to be in foal. You will also need to decide whether you are intending to transport the mare to and from the stallion for each covering or intend leaving her at the stud to be covered until she has 'gone off'. If you are leaving her, it is a very good idea to find out what the charge for keeping the mare will be right at the start, in order not to get a nasty shock when you arrive to collect her. Most stallion owners are extremely fair about their charges for keeping visiting mares; however, there are the few who are not, so it is always wise to check.

The right time to take your mare to stud depends on your personal circumstances. If you take your mare to stud in May, you will have a foal in April. In the United Kingdom, as the weather can be unpredictable in April, I prefer to cover my mares in late May, early June. That way the foals have a better chance of the weather beginning to settle.

Some breeders like to have very early foals as they are then well ahead of the rest growth-wise for early showing. We always foal our mares indoors in large foaling boxes so that there are no problems, but if the mares are kept stabled they should be exercised every day, weather permitting. One disadvantage of having very early foals is that if the mare is to foal outside she can produce a foal in the middle of the night and the poor little soul is forced to spend its first few hours on this earth fighting off the elements, and in some cases, losing the battle. Another disadvantage of early foals is that, if you

intend showing your foal, it will look good during the early shows and possibly win you prizes, being more advanced than the other exhibits, but halfway through the season it will begin to look like a yearling, losing its foal-like prettiness, thus ending up down the line against the foals it has already beaten earlier in the season.

When a mare goes to stud her shoes must be removed, for obvious reasons. Also it is advisable to have your mare insured, as accidents can and do unfortunately happen even in the best of studs and the results can prove costly. Your mare should be in a good physical condition and – very importantly – well wormed, when you take her to stud. It is a well-known fact amongst breeders that the condition of the mare can affect conception. It is imperative that the mare's condition and bodyweight are maintained and she should be neither too overweight nor too underweight. Taking a fat, unfit mare to stud is not advisable as she may prove very difficult, if not impossible, to get in foal.

CHAPTER FIVE

SHOWING IN-HAND

In-hand showing is a useful method not only of showing your stock to the potential buyer, who is watching to see if your animals are the type they would like to own themselves, but also of giving your future performance animals experience in ring craft and travelling. Whether you win or not, the benefits of showing the youngster are well worth the effort of taking a young horse to a show before it is old enough to be broken in, as this experience can make the job of further training much simpler. An added bonus is that if you stand your own stallion at stud and his stock are seen to be in the ribbons, the more mares you will get to him.

Showing in-hand is also within the capabilities of a wider range of exhibitors than ridden showing. Those who may not be as successful as they would wish in ridden showing for one reason or another, find that in-hand showing has more to offer them. The world of in-hand showing also has much to offer the older exhibitors who wish to continue in the ring, but now find ridden showing just a little too much for them: they can find much to enjoy in the more relaxed and less demanding in-hand classes. There are also others who could become involved quite unintentionally when they have bred from a favourite mare that for some reason is no longer suitable for riding.

The most important rule of any form of showing is that your animals must be in tip-top condition. Years ago you could bring something out of the field one day and show it the next day and win, but those days are long gone. The standard has become very high and is rising, and competition for honours is fierce. Mares should be brought in from grass at the end of December, the beginning of January at the latest, in order to have them ready in proper condition for the shows. Having said that I do not approve of keeping any horse permanently stabled for months on end, especially mares that are in foal, and so they should be turned out for an hour or so each day to exercise themselves and relieve the boredom whenever the weather allows.

Any form of showing, either in-hand or under saddle, is an art in itself and it takes time to learn all the tricks of the trade. Presentation is the all important factor. You may own the near perfect specimen – the perfect horse or pony has yet to be born – but if you do not present it correctly, it will not win. Whereas, the animal with a fault or two, which can be disguised by clever presentation, could be on top. Also, it is not only the turnout of the animal that counts, but of the handler as well. It is no earthly use showing an immaculately turned out horse or pony with an unkempt and scruffy handler running by the side.

Showing in-hand is the breeder's shop window. A long list of in-hand winnings will put value onto an animal, provided they are not all gained under the same judge: it will read well in an advertisement and will consequently impress some potential customers. However, some may be wary, as what wins as a foal with the breeder, will not necessarily win with the purchaser the following year. Also some buyers of future ridden prospects often prefer to buy something which is completely untouched, so it is often a question of swings and roundabouts.

It is never a good idea to show foals and youngsters too much, so if you are the type of person who wishes to go to every single show you can possibly get to, you will need to have a number of youngsters ready in show condition in order to alternate their outings. Showing a youngster two or three times in a week, and indeed showing the same animal every week over a long period of time, is a recipe for disaster as the animal can become stale and lose that vital spark that has made him a winner.

Over-showing is not the road to travel down. The youngster's developing limbs can be put under a great deal of strain whilst travelling around the country, especially when adjusting their balance around corners, and no matter how carefully you drive, you cannot avoid this. Also, loading and unloading, which takes great effort, and stopping and starting can also cause great strain to young limbs.

Over-showing can also lead to boredom. Horses can stop dead in the ring and refuse to move another step if staleness has set in. They can also become nappy and ring shy, neither of which traits are conducive to producing a champion ridden prospect, as that all important ingredient of a champion, presence, could be lost forever during that first season of showing a foal.

Over-feeding is as bad as over-showing. Nowadays breeders have a tendency to push so much feed into their animals, in order to get them into what they consider to be show condition, that not only do they look mature far beyond their age, but some of the in-hand classes around the country tend to be more like fat stock classes than showing ones. Over-feeding can cover up some bad points, but it can never change a bad specimen into a good one. However, not all the blame can be put upon the breeder and exhibitor as, unfortunately, there are some judges around who prefer animals to look this way and put them at the top of the line. This does little to help the breeders and producers who feed their animals sensibly, leaving them no option other than not to show under these particular judges.

Feeding too much hard feed into a foal leads to the animal becoming over large and too mature-looking for its age. In breeding circles these animals are called 'bucket foals'. Misleadingly for the unaware, they can be prolific winners in their foal year, but are not exhibited as yearlings. The reason for this is that they have gone completely 'off' and no way would they be in the ribbons. They may never be shown in the ring again at any age as their showing career has been ruined for life. Ask the exhibitor of a 'bucket foal' why he isn't showing it as a yearling and he will come up with every excuse under the sun why it is not out that year. But the sad truth is that it was overdone as a foal and spoiled: it is no longer suitable for showing, at least in its yearling year, and possibly for ever. So, although showing your young stock most certainly has its advantages, be aware that there is a downside as well. Moderation in all things should be the name of the showing game, and surely the ultimate accolade for you, the breeder, is to have an animal you have bred win at Wembley in later years, rather than winning a pile of ribbons as a youngster. After all, your prime concern as a breeder should be to breed quality that will ensure the future of the breed.

When producing mares and foals for the show ring, bearing in mind that each horse is an individual, plan a nutritious feeding system with plenty of protein, vitamins and minerals. Using a feed balancer with some alfalfa chaff is also good, and of course, good quality hay or haylage is essential. A bran mash once a week is also a good idea. Feeding is up to the individual owner but do take care not to get carried away and over-feed as it is more difficult to eradicate those pads of fat that have mysteriously appeared before your eyes due to excess food and lack of exercise, than it is to put weight on. Also essential is a regular worming programme: it is of no use whatever to feed your animals for worms to have the benefit. Mares should be wormed every six weeks, and foals can be safely wormed at six weeks old and every following six weeks afterwards.

Foals will be fine having only their mother's milk for the first six weeks, and will most likely be well into eating solids by then in any case. Most foals will begin eating solid food around a week old and sometimes less with their mothers. If you find the mare is holding her foal back from the feed, it is best to have a separate manger for the youngster to feed from and to keep the mare tied up until the foal has finished, to make certain it gets adequate rations.

Halter the foal when it is a few days old, preferably with a leather foal slip as these easily break if caught up, and teach it to lead alongside its mother. At the same time you should teach it to walk freely alongside you, neither dragging back or trailing behind you. Foals should be taught to think forward going. You will be surprised how quickly it will catch on. Also getting the foal used to standing correctly, being brushed and having it's feet picked up early on saves problems later. The more the foal learns in the beginning, the better it will go in the ring when the time comes. It will pay dividends to make sure that your exhibits will stand, walk out and trot on correctly without breaking, before you even contemplate entering a show.

When you go to a show leave home early to ensure that you do not have to drive like a maniac in order to get there with plenty of time before your class. Personally I like to arrive at a show at least one and a half hours before the class; that way nobody gets stressed out – including the animals.

Having thoroughly washed and dried your exhibit the night before the show, try to complete most of your grooming before leaving home so that you should only have the final polishing, chalking socks and oiling hooves left to do when you arrive. Do make sure that everything is spot on and that includes yourself and your foal handler if you are showing a foal.

You are unlikely to win many ribbons, if any, if your exhibits are immaculate and you, the exhibitor, are not. Every judge likes to see a combination before him that pleases his eye, which means that the horse and the handler should complement one another, and not detract from one another.

Choose your showing outfit carefully. Your clothes should tone in with your exhibit, not clash with it, and certainly not be so eye-catching that they detract completely from your animal. Something plain and simple is the answer. In the Welsh Cob classes a neat, subdued coloured pair of trousers, not jeans, a smart shirt and tie, a waistcoat or tweed jacket if the weather is cold, and a pair of smart discreetly coloured trainers – white ones are alright if they *are* white, but not if they are a muddy shade of grey – will be suitable. I feel obliged here to quote a gentleman who shall be nameless, writing in a well-known horse magazine about dress for handlers. This gentleman stated that trainers were totally unsuitable to be worn in showing classes, and he actually gave as an example the handlers of Welsh Cob Stallions. I can only assume that this gentleman had never had the experience of attempting to run a Welsh Cob Stallion in a pair of leather jodhpur boots! Although I hasten to add that although also suitable for the Section C classes, trainers are not suitable footwear for the Section B classes where a smart pair of jodhpur boots are *de rigueur*. A jacket is essential, and also a hat for the Section B classes.

If you are showing a mare and foal it is preferable for your foal handler to be dressed the same as yourself; this makes for a co-ordinated look and fills the judge's eye with a neat and professional picture. A word here about the ladies' hairdos. Keep your hair neat and tidy: nothing looks worse than long hair blowing around in the wind, so if it is long, tie it up with something dark-coloured and unobtrusive, not, please, with half a dozen different coloured scrunchies which resemble Christmas decorations.

When showing in-hand you have to be 'on the

ball' at all times. When you enter the ring come in at a brisk walk or trot, whichever suits your particular animal, making sure it is alert and not trailing into the ring, dragging its feet. First impressions are usually the ones that stay in the mind of the judge throughout the class. When walking round the ring initially, keep walking at a brisk, alert walk. When asked to stand to wait your turn to trot round make sure your horse is standing four square and ready to take off at a brisk trot when your turn comes; also make sure you do not break into canter half way round the ring. A horse that continually breaks cannot move out and show off its paces as it should do. When all the individual shows are finished, keep your horse walking round briskly, keeping an eye on the judge so as to be ready when you are called into line, going into line straightaway when signalled. Again, make certain your horse is standing four square with its head up when standing in line, keeping your horse attentive and alert, ready for when you are called out in front of the judge.

Stand your horse up in front of the judge on the nearside, making sure it is standing four square, but in the case of Section Bs, with the near fore slightly in front of the off fore and the near hind just behind the off hind, so that the judge can see all four legs and not just two. Make sure the overall picture you present to the judge is one of scope and presence. If your horse is short-coupled you can make him stand out, but if he is a little bit long in the back try not to spread him out, making the picture look even longer. When asked to walk out make sure you walk in a straight line at a brisk walk for as long as you can, as the further you walk away, the further you have to trot back to the judge giving him plenty of time to see that your horse moves straight and also time to bring him down to a trot if he should break into canter. When you turn your horse always turn it away from you, do not drag it round towards you – it could step on your toes! When you have turned completely and are back in a straight line, ask your horse to trot at a brisk trot past the judge and around the arena, back into line. When trotting out always look ahead, occasionally looking down and checking that your feet are in tune with your horse, and landing at the same time as your horse's front feet. Be alert when standing in line, make sure your horse is four square and looking interested, and if asked to go out for a final walk round make sure your horse is still looking lively as this could be the critical stage: you could go up the line, but if your horse is slopping along at this stage you could just as easily go down. When called back in the final line-up be on the ball and keep your horse alert. Until the rosettes are actually given out the judge could still change his mind so it pays to be vigilant.

If you are showing in a mare and foal class the judge will call the foals in for judging after the mares are finished. This is the moment that all your hard work and training at home pays off. The foal should walk into the middle of the ring quite independently of its mother, and you should not have to either drag it forward or to hold it back. It should have a nice, alert, free walk, and be happy to walk alongside you, it should not be jumping around like a 'jack in the box' and falling about on the floor in temper. Young stock require more attention in the ring than adults as they are not as balanced as older, more experienced stock and can also 'spook' at the least little thing. For this reason it is a good idea to have a fairly long lead with a foal so that if it pulls away from you, you can give it a little slack rather then allow it to pull against you.

Foals need more sympathetic handling than older stock and you should keep them at a steadier pace when trotting out as they are more likely to break into a canter or to stop dead. With practice at home before the show you will know exactly what pace suits your particular animal to show it off to its best advantage.

If your foal is not going well on its own by the first show, you can, of course, have your handler lead the mare around the ring in front of it so that it will trot out, but do make sure the mare is in front and not alongside the foal thus detracting from the picture that the judge wants to see.

With young stock it is always better to walk briskly for a few strides before asking it to trot out giving the animal time to keep its balance, trotting slowly at first so that it gains its balance and activity from behind, then trot out keeping in a straight line.

Do not turn you animal's head towards you, nor away from you, as both these positions are incorrect.

Always teach your in-hand animals to stand still in the line-up. There is nothing worse than a foal or youngster who simply will not stand still. The other animals in the line-up become fidgety and worse still can start kicking and cavorting around, thus upsetting the whole line. If this happens you most certainly will not endear yourself to the judge who could ask you to leave the ring altogether if your animal cannot behave itself; it could also become a danger to others.

When showing the Welsh Breeds there are different rules in the various Sections governing the headgear that animals are shown in when competing in the in-hand classes. All stallions should be shown in a leather bridle with a stallion bit with horses shoes, a brass chain and a leather lead. Mares in Section D, Section C, and in the Welsh Mountain classes should be shown in a clean, white, halter. However some people do show Welsh Mountain mares in a narrow leather bridle without a bit. In the Section B classes all stock are shown in leather bridles or, in the case of foals, in fine, leather headcollars. It goes without saying that all your leatherwork should be in good condition, clean and polished, with any brass parts gleaming. In the female youngstock classes in Sections D, Sections C and Section A, all ages should be shown in white halters.

CHAPTER SIX

THE WELSH BREEDS IN RIDDEN SHOWING

There are suitable classes in ridden showing to accommodate all age groups and all the four Sections of the Welsh Breeds.

SHOWING THE WELSH MOUNTAIN PONY AND THE WELSH PONY

The Welsh Mountain Pony, Section A, and the Welsh Pony, Section B, with their kind and sensible temperament and exceptionally pretty looks, both make excellent ridden show ponies for children.

The Welsh Mountain Pony is ideally suited to the ambitious smaller child, as he not only excels in the Leading Rein and First Ridden classes, but he is also so nimble that he is capable of jumping either coloured or natural obstacles and so makes a superb, game little hunter, a cradle-stakes and nursery-stakes pony as well.

The Welsh Pony, Section B, the latest addition to the Stud Book, came about due to the need for a bigger, quality riding pony for young people that could take its place alongside the thoroughbreds in the show ring. The Section B was originally arrived at by crossing the Welsh Mountain pony with a small Cob, but so great was the demand for quality riding ponies the Welsh Pony was upgraded by selective breeding to produce the elegance and quality we find today. With the result that today, the Section B and part-bred Section B, not only takes its place in the show pony and working hunter pony classes with enormous success, he also makes an elegant harness pony and a sure-footed mounted-games prospect. Today the basic Welsh structure still remains the same, the characteristic head and eye, the good angle to the jaw, the big shoulder and good length of rein, with strong legs and feet.

SUITABLE CLASSES
THE LEADING REIN CLASS

The Leading Rein classes are best suited to the Welsh Mountain Pony as opposed to the Welsh Pony, though there are occasionally some very small-bred Section Bs among the exhibits. I would advise against these miniature show ponies as they can tend to be flighty and have far too extravagant an action which can unseat a tiny jockey, possibly putting the child off riding, or at the very least showing, for the rest of its life. The Welsh Mountain Pony has a far steadier temperament and is the much safer ride for the tiny child. At some of the bigger shows the classes are divided into two sections: ponies up to 11.2hh (117 cms) and over 11.2hh (117 cms) to 12hh (122 cms). These classes are for riders up to and including seven years of age and so cater for the various sizes of small children. Ponies must be four years-old and over.

The competition is fierce in the leading rein classes and the standard extremely high so to do well you need a top class combination of pony and jockey. The first rule is that the jockey should fit the pony. It is of no use having a pony up to full height if your jockey is so tiny that the legs are way above the saddle flaps, neither is it any good having a dainty, small pony with an over-large jockey whose feet are almost trailing along the floor. The judge wants to see a pleasing combination that fits together nicely, and is going well.

A leading rein pony should not only have good paces, it should be unflappable and it should have perfect manners at all times. However, to be successful it should not be a slug, but should show plenty of presence. It should walk out freely, but not too fast, and its trot should be well extended but also steady and controlled. It should be willing and obedient: when asked to go from walk to trot it should change pace quietly, and come back from trot to walk easily. No judge wants to see a flighty

pony with a tiny jockey clinging on for dear life because the pony is cavorting around the ring. Ponies with this type of temperament are not suitable as leading rein ponies. The perfect leading rein pony should be quiet at all times, and should stand in line like a rock, not moving for any reason; even if the pony next in line is playing up it should not copy it. There are some judges who might ask the larger child to dismount and lead the pony a short way to prove that it is suitable for a child to handle; also, the larger child will be expected to mount unaided to show that the pony is patient and quiet. In the Leading Rein classes a tiny jockey is not expected to be much more than a passenger in the saddle. However, the larger child can be expected to have some control over the pony which should respond to the rider's aids and should not attempt to go charging off.

When showing in Leading Rein classes not only should the jockey fit the pony, but they should also visually complement one another, as should the rider and the leader. For example some years ago I showed a golden dun pony in Leading Rein classes. First of all I tried a navy blue and pale blue colour scheme which looked nice but not outstanding, so I changed to brown and orange, and the transformation was unbelievable. The blue colour scheme had the effect of making the pony's coat look a paler shade of dun, whereas the brown and orange deepened it into a strong golden shade. A lot of thought should go into the colour scheme of the rider's clothes to bring out the best in, and not detract from, the pony.

The leader should follow the colour scheme of the rider and should be smart, but the current trend of the ladies wearing outfits resembling wedding outfits makes them look quite ridiculous, especially when such ladies are seen teetering around on high-heeled shoes, sometimes getting stuck in the mud, hanging permanently on to their wide-brimmed, flower-festooned hats with one hand in case they blow away with the first slight puff of wind. These ladies remind me of over-decorated, animated Christmas trees. A plain, neat trouser suit with a blouse the same colour as the browband looks far smarter, with a pair of jodhpur boots below, and if you must wear a hat, choose a plain one with a small brim: a neat trilby is ideal. Neat but workmanlike should be the aim.

In the Leading Rein classes the first impression the judge has is of the combination in front of him, that is the pony, the rider who fits the pony exactly, and the handler all turned out to perfection and in matching harmony. He will then be looking for a pony which is alert and has presence, who is walking along willingly but is not flighty, who is steady and easily controllable at both the walk and the trot, and who stands in line like a rock.

The First Ridden class is the first of the riding classes off the leading rein. The pony must be four years-old or over, not exceeding 12.0hh (122 cms), suitable for a rider ten years and under. In this class

the jockey has to be able to ride competently off the leading rein at all paces, and so finding the right pony for the jockey is extremely important. A first ridden pony should go forward freely, be capable of smooth transitions, and, as cantering is expected in this class, the pony should have good steering and brakes. Manners are extremely important as this is the first time the jockey is riding independently; however, no judge likes to see a child continually kicking into their pony to make it go forward. He wants to see a pony with some presence and not one that drags itself around the ring half asleep. Here again, the Welsh Mountain Pony is a much better choice than a small Section B. The elegant and pretty miniature thoroughbred behaving like an unexploded firework is not the type the judge will be looking for in this class. In the eyes of the judge the Welsh Mountain Pony will look, and will be, a safe, confidence-giving pony who will not only give the jockey a pleasant ride around the ring in a show but will also give the child many hours of pleasure riding alone at home.

Here the judge will be looking for a quiet, steady, confidence-giving, easily-controlled pony at all paces, a pony that goes forward when asked by his jockey, but who also stops with no trouble when asked. He does not want to see a pony that is too sharp and who anticipates his rider, nor one that is a slug and who takes a lot of persuading to change pace. He wants to see that the jockey is in control and has to ask the pony to do things, which the pony does willingly but never does more than he is asked.

RIDING PONY NOT EXCEEDING 12.2HH (128 CMS).
FOUR YEARS-OLD AND OVER. RIDER 13 YEARS AND UNDER

The Welsh Mountain Pony or the smaller bred Section B pony are both suitable in size for this class. However, you should bear in mind that the chubby little native pony is not what the judges are looking for, although it is generally agreed that the 12.2hh pony should show more native blood than the larger show ponies. Welsh Mountain ponies have been known to win this class but you have to have an exceptional one to beat a top class 12.2hh Section B pony.

As with previous classes, the rider should fit the pony. On average, most thirteen year-olds are too large to fit a 12.2hh pony and some twelve and eleven year-olds can be too large as well. If your jockey is larger and taller than average it is best to leave this class alone and go on to the next one: the pony with a jockey whose feet are close to the ground will not be a suitable combination. However, if you have an experienced jockey who fits a 12.2hh pony nicely go ahead and enter.

The jockey in this class should be an experienced rider, able to get the best out of the pony. The pony should be well-schooled, have impeccable manners and should be responsive to the aids of the rider at all paces. He should show quality and have perfect manners at all times. Ponies in this class are not only expected to give a far more sophisticated performance than the ones in previous classes, they will also be expected to gallop in this class and the judge will be unlikely to forgive even a hint of bad manners.

RIDING PONY EXCEEDING 12.2HH (128 CMS) NOT EXCEEDING 13.2HH (138 CMS). FOUR YEARS-OLD AND OVER.
RIDERS 14 YEARS AND UNDER

This is the class where the finer bred type of Welsh Pony, Section B, comes into his own. The 13.2hh class often contains some of the finest examples of the riding pony and the Section B is the finest of the pure-bred native breeds. Having said this, the class is, of course, also suitable for the part-bred Welsh riding pony. As the ponies in this class are large enough, you should see them give a really polished, sophisticated performance with their professional jockeys. They should be full of quality and elegance, and yet small enough to retain their pony character, which is most important. Here the combination element should be taken very seriously indeed as the wrong size, or inexperienced jockey, can present an imbalanced picture to the judge. For this class anything less than all-round perfection just will not do.

Again, as with all other classes, manners are still

all important. How often have you seen mothers on top of show ponies cantering them round in circles behind the lorries for an hour before the class to eliminate the fizz? To my mind any pony that needs to be ridden by an adult before the jockey climbs aboard is not fit to be called a 'child's pony' and I often wonder what would happen to these ponies in the ring if the judge had seen them being ridden in before the class.

RIDING PONIES EXCEEDING 13.2 HH (138 CMS)
BUT NOT EXCEEDING 14.2HH (148 CMS). FOUR YEARS-OLD AND OVER.
RIDERS 16 YEARS AND UNDER

This is the class in which the part-bred Section B pony excels. The key word in this class is riding *pony* which means the judge wants to see an animal in front of him with pony character and not a miniature hack. A miniature hack without pony blood should not be able to win a pony class and fortunately judges in general, though unfortunately not all, recognise this.

The 14.2hh pony should, as with all the other show-pony sizes, have impeccable manners and should be a free-going, bold and balanced ride. His transitions should be smooth and effortless, should neither hot up, nor look as if he has no enthusiasm. He should show that he is well able to gallop, but he should never hot up at the gallop and should ooze presence at all times. Again, combination is all important, the jockey must fit the pony to fill the judge's eye with a picture of elegance.

WORKING HUNTER PONIES

The working hunter pony must be beautiful, kind, free-moving, substantial and fast. He also needs to be willing, bold, clever and agile. The ideal working hunter pony must show the quality of a pony, the looks and substance of a small hunter and the performance of a working hunter. He should be obedient and schooled in his paces, should be straight, correct and sound. His gaits should be long, level, smooth and free and have a swinging, active walk, a long-striding regular trot, a comfortable, balanced canter and a naturally long, low gallop. Over fences he must be a careful and bold performer, clever enough to get himself out of a difficult situation, easily controllable and able to perform at a good hunting pace.

His conformation will be heavier than that of the show pony in every way. He should have more bone and substance, a plainer head and have a more workmanlike appearance and action. He should not be coarse, but he should not be pretty. He should be handsome and personable, and if he is to be a success in the ring he must have that bit of extra presence and quality to make him stand out above the crowd. In the smaller working hunter pony classes the Welsh Pony, Section B, is definitely in his element and extremely difficult to beat. In the larger classes the part-bred Section B is the best overall contender.

THE WORKING HUNTER PONY CLASSES

Working hunter pony. Open cradle stakes. Pony four years-old and over, not exceeding 12.0hh (122 cms). Rider 10 years-old and under.

Working hunter pony. Open nursery stakes. Ponies four years-old and over, not exceeding 13hh (133 cms). Rider 12 years and under.

Working hunter pony. Four years-old and over, not exceeding 13.hh (133 cms). Rider 14 years and under.

Working hunter pony four years-old and over. Exceeding 13hh (133 cms) but not exceeding 14hh (143 cms). Rider 16 years and under.

Working hunter pony four years-old and over. Exceeding 14hh (143 cms) but not exceeding 15hh (153 cms). Rider 19 years and under.

Whatever the height of the pony the requirements for the above classes remain the same. He has to be the right size for the jockey and temperamentally suitable. An excitable temperament is quite unsuitable, as the perfect hunting pony should never hot up and he should enjoy his jumping. The first part of any working hunter class is the jumping for which half of the total marks can be achieved, the other half for conformation and performance. In these classes you will be required to gallop in your ridden show, and will also be required to show your pony in-hand.

SHOW HUNTER PONIES

This is purely a ridden class with no jumping phase. The type of pony required is the same as for the working hunter pony classes. Type is important and the Section B is the correct type of pony to win these classes. The pony should have good conformation, he must move correctly and straight. He should be obedient and forward-going at all times without pulling or going on too fast. Overbending, going with his head in the air and his back hollow, and similar faults would all be penalised. He should demonstrate a correct outline at all times, and there should be no faults, such as a dipped back, revealed by removing his saddle.

SHOW HUNTER PONY CLASSES

Mare or gelding four years-old or over, not exceeding 12hh 122 cms. Riders not to have attained their 11th birthday before 1st January in the current year.

Mare or gelding four years-old or over, exceeding 122 cms, but not exceeding 133 cms. Riders not to have attained their 14th birthday before 1st January in the current year.

Mare or gelding four years-old or over, exceeding 133 cms but not exceeding 143 cms. Riders not to have attained their 17th birthday before 1st January in the current year.

Mare or gelding four years-old or over, exceeding 143 cms, but not exceeding 153 cms. Riders not to have attained their 20th birthday before 1st January in the current year.

RIDDEN MOUNTAIN AND MOORLAND CLASSES

The Welsh Mountain Pony, the Welsh Pony of Cob Type, and the Welsh Cob are all in their element in the Mountain and Moorland classes and are strong contenders for the honours. Several of them have qualified for Wembley and won there more than once. As with any of the other showing classes the rider must fit the pony; an unsuitable combination will not do justice to either the jockey or the animal and, again, as with all the other classes, manners do count. A badly-mannered pony is bound to lose points in the final judging however beautiful it may look.

SUITABLE CLASSES

Leading rein pony, registered mare or gelding, four years-old or over not exceeding 12.hh (122 cms). Registered in the stud books of Welsh Sections A and B, Dartmoor, Exmoor, Shetland and New Forest. Riders 9 years-old and under. Ponies to be shown in snaffle bridles on a leading rein.

Stallion, mare or gelding, four years-old or over. Registered in the stud books of Welsh A and B, Dartmoor, Exmoor and Shetland. Rider any age.

Suitable classes for the Welsh Pony of Cob Type

Section C and the Welsh Cob, section D under saddle.

RIDDEN MOUNTAIN AND MOORLAND

Stallion, mare or gelding, four years-old or over and registered in the stud books of Welsh C and D, Connemara, New Forest, Dales, Fells and Highland. Rider any age.

WORKING HUNTER PONY CLASSES

Working hunter pony, four years-old and over, exceeding 13hh (133 cms) and not exceeding 14hh (143 cms). Rider 17 years and under.

Working hunter pony exceeding 14hh (143 cms) and not exceeding 15hh (153 cms). Rider 20 years and under.

WELSH PONY OF COB TYPE, SECTION C

Stallion, mare or gelding, four years-old or over to be ridden and judged as a riding horse at a walk, trot, canter and gallop.

WELSH COB, SECTION D

Welsh Cob stallion, four years-old and over to be ridden and judged as a riding horse at a walk, trot, canter and gallop.

Welsh Cob mare or gelding, four years-old or over to be ridden and judged as a riding horse at a walk, trot, canter and gallop.

In the Mountain and Moorland classes the Welsh

Pony of Cob Type, Section C, and the Welsh Cob, Section D, if produced correctly, with a jockey of suitable size and experience, are without doubt, the strongest contenders of the native breeds and should always be at the top of these classes.

In the Working Hunter Pony classes the Welsh Cob, Section D, again comes into his own as an extremely strong contender for the top placings. The Welsh Pony of Cob Type, Section C, can also do well in these classes provided he is of the breeding of the 'true pony type' and not of the small Welsh Cob type on four legs which some breeders tend to prefer.

The Welsh Cob and the Section C are probably the most versatile of all the native breeds and have been renowned for centuries for their handsome appearance, strength, quality and spectacular movement. Always superb trotters, they are fantastic performers. The Section C is a superb ride-and-drive animal, up to weight and ideal as a mount to bridge the gap for young people between the pony and the horse.

CHAPTER SEVEN

PRODUCTION AND RINGCRAFT

PRODUCTION

No matter what sections of the Welsh Breeds you intend to show, in whatever showing classes, the importance of skilful production is paramount. It goes without saying that you should have a top-class animal to win a class, but skilful production can hide a multitude of sins.

First and foremost it is what goes inside that counts most, and good feeding is an art which takes experience and time to perfect. Condition and bloom come from within and if an animal is not fed well he will not gain the necessary condition to win a show. Feeding is a question of balance, the correct amount of food to suit the animal's bodyweight and the right balance of vitamins, minerals and protein to keep him feeling and looking healthy, and in tip-top condition. As already said, feeding is an art and it is a mistake to think that the larger the feed the better condition the animal will be in. Quality, not quantity is what counts and too much quantity can be a recipe for disaster; also, take care that the amount of protein you feed is not over the top. Some owners swear by feeding large amounts of protein to their animals, and the end result could mean protein poisoning. Horse shows are not fat-stock shows as so many exhibitors today seem to think: an animal with pads of fat wobbling about as it goes round the ring is not a pretty sight and not likely to be in the running for the ribbons. So, feed enough to keep your exhibit nicely covered but not excessively so. The make and type of feed you use is a matter for individual choice and what suits your animals best, but do make sure that they have plenty of good hay or haylage, and water always available as well as hard feed.

Most essential for a stabled animal is adequate exercise. Show animals should be brought into the stable in late December to get them ready and in show condition by the start of the showing season in the spring. Weather permitting they should either be turned out for a short while each day to stretch their legs or, if your fields and paddocks are not in a fit state to turn anything out into, they should be exercised in-hand or ridden out for a short while daily. Horses that are kept stabled without adequate exercise are not happy animals and all sorts of problems can occur through boredom alone, not to mention the possible side effects to your animal's health.

At the start of the show season, assuming that

your potential exhibits are fit, healthy and ready to compete, it will be time to trim them for their respective classes. The Welsh Breeds require very little trimming for the In-Hand classes. The only parts that should need trimming will be the whiskers and the tail. The whiskers should be removed and the tail trimmed both at the top to make it tidy, and at the bottom. In the In-hand and Native classes the tail should be trimmed to just below the hock and not cut into a straight line, but layered to look natural. There is nothing that looks worse on a Native animal than a tail that is cut straight across the bottom, or a tail which is so long – even in some cases, trailing along the ground – that it prevents the judge from getting a clear view of the animal's hindquarters and hocks, and worse still can have the effect of making your animal look light of bone. The mane can be pulled slightly to tidy it up if it is very uneven or over-thick, but this should only be done slightly as pulled manes are incorrect: one plait, not turned under, can be put in behind the ear. Also, in the Native classes, which include all the Ridden Native classes as well as the In-hand ones, the feathers are never trimmed, everything being left as natural as possible. However, if your animal is what is termed as 'rough behind', meaning that the feather extends up the hindlegs to near the hock, then some judicious trimming is required to give him a clean outline on the legs.

In the Ridden Showing classes, that is the Leading Rein Show class and the Riding Pony classes, different rules apply, as they do also for exhibitors of Welsh Part-Bred Horses in Hunter and Riding Horse breeding classes.

For the Leading Rein Show classes the ponies should have their manes and tails pulled and trimmed, and the fetlocks are also trimmed. When trimming use hand clippers instead of scissors, as you have to be very clever and experienced with the scissors in order not to make unsightly marks. The tail can be plaited for these classes if you so wish, but I personally think that a neat and well-pulled tail looks far nicer. The mane should always be plaited.

Clever plaiting can improve the neck line. If the pony is inclined to be cresty, tight plaits which sit below the crest line will make him look less so, and if he needs more, crest-high plaits which sit on top of the neck will give the impression of extra. Try to pull the mane so that it is of an even length and thickness all along the neck, that the plaits will all be of even size. Nothing looks worse or less professional than lumpy and uneven plaits. There is no strict ruling as to the number of plaits you should put in, and if your pony lacks in the length of his neck the more plaits you put in the better as this has the effect of making his neck look longer. Less plaits, of course, will shorten the neck. Always sew in the plaits, making sure they are tight and secure, and all of the same size and thickness, if possible; *never* use elastic bands for plaiting in showing classes. If there are any stray ends when you have finished plaiting this is *not* the time to grab the scissors; it is better to hold the stray ends in place and use a strong holding hairspray or clear hair gel to keep them down.

It goes without saying that your animal should be squeaky clean and polished to perfection, with perfectly whitened socks if applicable and, of course, nicely oiled hoofs. Quarter marks can be used in the Leading Rein, Section B and Part-Bred Riding classes and they are not just useful for decoration. If your horse or pony tends to have a bit of a hollow flank and his second thigh is a little weak, sharks' teeth will effectively fill in the flanks and make the second thigh look stronger; also, brush marks make the quarters look stronger. For the finishing touches you should discreetly highlight the eyes, nostrils and muzzle with Vaseline, liquid paraffin or baby oil and brush some Brilliantine into the tail.

For the Welsh Part-Bred classes horses should be plaited and can also have discreet quarter marks. Discreet trimming of the head and heels is permissible and tails should be plaited or pulled and levelled.

For travelling to and from a show your stock should be well-bandaged in order to avoid injury to precious limbs, and rugged up with a light travelling sheet if the weather is hot or a thicker travelling rug if it is cold, to keep them clean and comfortable. The horsebox or trailer should be well-bedded down to lessen any risk of injury and if it is a hot

day be sure to make certain the trailer is well ventilated. Careful driving is essential, especially when going around corners, so that you avoid unnecessary strain on the animal's legs. A steady, sensible speed is also advisable which, hopefully, will avoid the need for sudden braking. When travelling long distances you should stop and check at regular intervals that your animals are safe and comfortable. A full haynet will give your horses something else to think about on the journey, but make sure it is securely tied and high enough so that the animal cannot get its feet or legs caught up in it.

Horseboxes and lorries should be thoroughly checked over at the start of the season and every so often through the season to make sure they are roadworthy and that the floors are sound and solid. It is not all that long ago that I was unfortunate enough to witness a horrific accident where a horse's legs had gone through the floor of a trailer. The animal's legs miraculously were not broken but the damage to its legs was so great, due to being dragged along underneath the trailer for some distance, that it had to be put down before being cut out of the trailer. I shall never forget seeing this poor horse desperately struggling to try to get out of the jockey door. The owner was in floods of tears but I am afraid I have to admit that I showed her no sympathy whatsoever. The accident was entirely her own fault: the trailer was totally unroadworthy, it was a lump of rust and literally falling to pieces. A responsible horse owner would have sent this trailer to the scrap years before.

It is of little use turning your exhibit out to perfection if your tack is not perfect to match. Dirty and ill-fitting tack is not only an insult to your animal but also an insult to the judge. The clever use of tack can not only improve on the appearance of an animal but can also help the jockey to give a better performance, making the animal a more comfortable and balanced ride. Also, if you are competing in a class where the judge is to ride the horses then the all-important first impression the judge gets when he mounts your animal, is a better one if your tack is correct and well-fitting. Just as certain items of tack can make an improvement on some of your animal's weaker points, unsuitable tack can just as easily highlight them.

In the Leading and First Ridden classes ponies are shown in a suitable bridle with a plain or coloured browband, and if you use a coloured one choose the colours carefully so that they enhance the colour of your pony, rather than detract from it. A pony with a small and very fine head will look better in a very narrow, possibly a rolled leather bridle which will show off its head to perfection, whereas the pony who has a not so fine, or slightly large head will benefit from a bridle of slightly wider leather which will give the impression of the head being smaller. A dainty, straightcut showing saddle will show off his shoulder and also have the effect of making his neck look longer. A good small showing saddle, which has a bit of depth to the seat,

to suit a tiny jockey, is worth its weight in gold, and if looked after will last for many years. However, remember it must also fit the pony, and without the need for a numnah which should not be used in a showing class. In the bigger classes a double bridle is the correct headgear and the same applies here as before, regarding the pony's head and width of the leather used. The same rules apply also for the saddle.

'Clothes maketh the man'. How true this is. It should go without saying that a perfectly turned-out pony should have a rider turned-out to match. It is the overall picture that the judge sees first and which catches his eye and the horse and the jockey must complement one another to make a pleasing combination, then giving the judge that all-important first impression. In all showing classes whether Ridden or In-Hand the rider or handler should be clean, neat, tidy, workmanlike, and unobtrusive. Choose the colour of your outfit to bring out the best in the colour of the animal and you will not go wrong.

RINGCRAFT

Expert showmanship is an art which can only be perfected through experience. An experienced showman can make a silk purse appear out of the proverbial sow's ear; in other words he can take a good but not necessarily outstanding animal and, by expert production, turn that animal into a Champion. Conversely, a bad showman will be unlikely to win, even with a potential Champion, as he has not perfected his craft. A good showman will have the know-how to produce an animal to perfection, make the most of its good points and be able to minimise its bad ones.

When you enter the ring your exhibit should be ready to show. You should not need to make two or three laps around the ring to reduce the fizz in him, but should have exercised him well and ensured he is going nicely along before the class is due to begin. While waiting in the collecting ring, size up your competitors to decide which one you want to follow into the ring. Ideally you do not want to enter behind an animal that is better than your own: place yourself in between two that are not as good so that your exhibit will stand out.

As the walk is the pace the judge will see first when you enter the ring, it is most important that your animal should walk out on an easy stride from the shoulder, with the hind legs well-engaged, going over the ground, not into it. A good walk indicates to the judge that the horse or pony will also have the ability to go well at all paces. If you find you are behind an animal that is jogging and nappy, or one that is sluggish and sloppy, do not stay behind spoiling your own animal's paces, but overtake quietly, keeping well away from the animals you are passing just in case one of them decides to take a kick at you. Good manners are an important part of a showing class so make absolutely certain your exhibit behaves impeccably at all times

and you could quite easily finish up ahead of an animal that is better than yours but which has not behaved itself.

Keep a close eye on the judge and the stewards so that when asked to move up a pace you do so smoothly with automatic transitions. At the trot it is important that the jockey rides on the correct diagonal otherwise the animal will look to be unbalanced. The trot should be rhythmic, balanced and smooth, with the animal flowing freely, being active, showing a good length of low level stride. He should be tracking up well, and should be neither too fast or choppy, and should not break into canter. When asked to canter do so smoothly at the next corner making certain you are on the correct leg, aiming to be in a clear space at the right time and not in a bunch, keeping in a clear space at all times to enable the judge to see you. The canter should be collected, going freely forward with the hocks well underneath and your horse or pony on the bit and not behind it. In some classes exhibitors are asked to gallop and if this is the case do make sure your animal does gallop and not just increase the speed of his canter. And when it is time to come back to walk your downward transitions should be gradual, exact and smooth.

Remain on the ball and attentive at all times and when called into line do so immediately and quietly, making sure your animal stands quietly, but does not fall asleep or rests a hindleg. Keep him alert and attentive at all times so that when you are called out to do your individual show he comes out of the line smartly and smoothly, looking alert and interested. Here the experienced and clever exhibitor will keep the show short and sharp, showing the animal off to its best advantage and covering up its weaknesses, using as much of the ring as you are allowed so that your transitions will be smooth and your circles will be a good shape. If he trots and canters on the right rein better than the left, work out your show so that you go round to the right rein. If he shows himself off better at the trot than the canter make your show mostly at the trot. If he has a good, free walk, make sure you make the best use of this at the beginning and end of your show. Remember that the closing stages of your individual show are the ones which remain in the judge's mind, so be sure to finish on a good note, making sure that your halt is square, your salute is neat and you smile pleasantly at the judge. Then go quietly back into line and maintain your animal's attention.

One most important point to remember in ridden showing is to look confident and happy at all times, thus giving the judge the impression that you know what you are doing, that your animal is a pleasure to ride, and you are enjoying yourself.

There is absolutely no point in producing your horse or pony to perfection if his manners are not up to standard. A beautifully-groomed pony and immaculately-dressed rider will not be in the ribbons if the animal is nappy, over-fresh, downright naughty or not correctly schooled. Time spent at home perfecting your exhibit's manners is time well spent, as also is time spent on the showground before your class working your animal in. Not only does the judge want to see a perfectly-mannered exhibit in the ring, in some of the ridden showing classes the judge will ride the animals himself and if your horse or pony does not stand still while he mounts, is bolshy about leaving the line-up, bucks and cavorts round the ring, does not have smooth transitions, and generally misbehaves, then the judge will most certainly not award him a ribbon.

Showing always has its ups and downs. You could be top of the line under one judge and halfway down or even at the bottom with another; so, whether you are on top or not, accept your placing with dignity, even if you feel you have been treated harshly.

CHAPTER EIGHT

PRESENT DAY STUDS IN THE UK

PENLLYN

One of the oldest established Welsh Mountain Pony studs in the UK, the Penllyn Stud was started in 1954 by Mrs Serena Homfray, and many prolific prizewinners have borne the Penllyn prefix and still do so today. The foundation ponies of the stud were bought in 1954 at the Cui dispersal sale from Mrs Betty Richards. They were the mares *Cui Phyllis* and *Cui Jane Ink*. Also in 1954, *Fayre Black Dawn* and *Fayre Skylark* were purchased from the Fayre Oaks Sale. In 1955 *Revel Bay Berry* joined the others and also the stallion, *Royal Reveller*. The FSI mare, *Cinderella*, who is the great grandmother of all the Penllyn ponies today, joined the stud in 1957.

Glascoed Mynydd was the beginning of the 'M' line. She produced a filly by *Clan Pip, Penllyn Mynydd Bach*, who later produced a filly named *Penllyn MA*, whose sire was *Woodend Prince*. *Myfanwy* produced *Penllyn Miranda*, by *Rookery Juniper*. *Miranda* had *Penllyn Melanie* and *Penllyn Melissa*, both by *Twyford Juggler*, and both prolific prizewinners. *Melissa*, born in 1983, won the Royal Welsh as a yearling, shown by Mrs Homfray who was then a 'young' seventy year-old. Today the stud has approximately twenty ponies which include two

stallions, the homebred *Penllyn Meurig*, by *Tullibardine Balsam*, and a stallion purchased at the Fayre Oaks Sale in 2000, the bay, *Fronbach Canny Lad [Synod Hello x Fronbach Cadi]*.

Mrs Homfray still runs the stud herself, a careful breeder, selling her stock mostly to private buyers, many of her ponies being exported to European countries and Australia. Mrs Homfray not only breeds excellent stock, but she also shows what she breeds and proves their quality by their prolific winnings.

HENIARTH

Heniarth Stud was formed in 1995 when Richard Miller and Meirion Davies moved to south-west Wales, close to Kidwelly. The prefix, registered in 1978, roughly translates as 'old farmyard'. Meirion was originally keen on his parents' Section B ponies; however, having a strong interest in Mountain Ponies, he secured *Marsh Marged Anne* who was dam of the first Heniarth animal back in 1978.

Initially interested in Cobs, Richard had been given the Section A mare, *Craven Ballerina*, so on returning from America he purchased her daughter, *Pendock Bobbin*, by *Twyford Juggler*, and having been impressed with the *Sunwillow* stock that he had the opportunity to show before moving Stateside, both he and Meirion selected *Sunwillow Yasmin* [*Pendock Legend* x *Sunwillow Quest*] as a foundation mare when she was a two year-old from the Forlan Stud. The opportunity to purchase *Yasmin*'s dam in the 1994 Fayre Oaks sale resulted in Richard and Meirion selling several other ponies, including *Pendock Bobbin,* so they were able to secure *Sunwillow Quest* [*Coed Coch Salsbri* x *Sunwillow Bernina*] for the world-record price of £4,500 gns. *Quest* became the cornerstone of the Heniarth stock. Her first foal, *Heniarth Quill* by *Maestir Valient* was gelded and has become an excellent ridden pony in the Midlands, winning at Leicester County two years running. Taking the chance to cover *Quest* with the unproven two year-old colt *Dukes Hill Magnum,* the blood of *Sunwillow Bernina [Marsh Crusader* x *Coed Coch Seren Wen* x *Coed Coch Siaradus]* was doubled up through *Magnum's* Dam, *Sunwillow Mutters [Revel Playsome* x *Sunwillow Fusshorn* by *Coed Coch Norman].* The result was *Heniarth Quip* who won the 1997 Royal Welsh yearling colt class and has since been Reserve Male Champion at the Royal of England and Shropshire & West Midlands as well as winning the Three Counties and the National Pony Show. During 2000 his first offspring hit the show ring collecting him over thirty points in the WPCS, sire ratings with two yearling fillies and a colt foal flying the flag. He has been patronised by some of the top studs in the Country, including Sunwillow, whose *Sunwillow Georgina* has collected many admirers.

Alongside their own stock Heniarth has welcomed some exceptional animals to produce for their owners, none more so than *Bryn-Odyn Scarlet* [*Pendock Legend* x *Dryfe Sheer Heaven*]. As a three year-old *Scarlet* was Native Pony Champion at the Royal of England and Wembley, winning the Templeton Qualifier at the Bath & West, and then going on to stand top Native in the pony final. As a brood mare in 1999 she stood Supreme Native Pony at the National Pony Show, taking the Wembley ticket, to eventually stand Reserve Pony of the Year.

Meirion Davies is currently on the WPCS Judges Panel for Sections A & B. Richard Miller was elected to the Council of the WPCS in 2000 and is currently on the Judges Panel for Sections A,B,C & D, also on the National Pony Society Judging Panels for mixed Mountain and Moorland breeds, Riding Pony Breeding and the Shetland Stud Book Society Judges Panel.

GELER

Having established the Geler prefix in the 1920s, the founder, David John Lloyd, passed it on to his son John who developed the present strain of Geler Welsh Cobs from 1946, and he in turn passed it on to his son William, who today runs it with his son, Gerallt. The Stud being located in the centre of Ceredigion Cob country, giving access to the prominent Cob stockgetters, went a long way to achieving the desired type of animal. The first Cob mare, *Geler Bess*, by *Brenin Gwalia*, produced *Geler Daisy* and *Geler Queen*, both by *Pentre Eiddwen Comet*, who both went on to be cornerstones in the development of the Welsh Cob in the 1950s.

Geler Daisy competed all the way at the Royal Welsh from 1954, gaining many placings, eventually winning the Female Championship in 1964. *Geler Queen*, the foundation mare of the Oakhatch Stud was 1965 Royal of England Female Champion. *Geler Daisy* produced *Geler Ann*, x *Cahn Dafydd*. Her full sister, *Geler Eirlys*, top price at the Llanarth Sale in 1971, was one of the Gerrig Stud's foundation mares.

Daisy's first colt of the 1960s was *Geler Macmillan*, x *Rhystud Prince*. The two colts by *Llanarth Braint* born in 1969 and 1970 topped the colt foals at the Llanarth Sales. Her last colt was *Geler Ifan Ho*, x *Tyhen Comet*. *Ifan Ho* achieved fame as a show horse, being successful at the Royal Welsh, and his blood still runs through the veins of the Welsh Cobs of today.

Geler Neli, born in 1969, x *Tyhen Comet*, is the present day matriarch of the Geler Stud although she passed away aged thirty years. *Neli* had two daughters, *Geler Brenhines* and *Geler Rosann*, both retained at home. Both had much success at all levels of shows and left females as well as sons, to breed from. *Neli* produced *Geler Cardi Model*, x *Derwen Rosina's Last*, *Geler Guto Goch*, x *Geler Ifan Ho*, *Geler Cardi Flyer*, x *Oakhatch Rowan*, and *Geler Carlo*, x *Parc Dafydd*, who is still at Geler today, a prolific show winner and a sire of many Royal Welsh winners. As a show mare, *Neli* reached the ultimate in 1977 as the Royal Welsh Female Champion.

In 2000 the young mares at Geler included *Twyosges, Miriam* and *Heti*, all expected to join *Sal, Rhiannon* and *Seren* as breeding mares. Of the stallions, *Derwen Desert Express* continues to do an excellent job, *Carlo*, still an active twenty year-old, whilst *Geler Dago,* x *Ystrad Dewi Victor*, many times a premium show winner, continues to sire exciting progeny for Geler.

GLEINANT

In 1982 Mrs Pauline Lloyd arrived at the Revel and purchased a four year-old grey/brown mare, *Revel Sepia* [*Rhiwa Titw* x *Revel Sepha* x *Twyford Grendadier*]. *Sepia* had a grey filly foal at foot, *Revel Sophie* (by *Knighton Fidello*) and was covered again by this same dun stallion. *Sepia* presented Pauline with a wonderful Palomino filly who was the first to bear the 'Gleinant' prefix. This was *Sequin*, who has the identical markings as her illustrious great-great-grand-dam' the 1957 Royal Welsh Champion *Revel Spring Song*. *Sequin* has bred some lovely stock including *Spangle* (at Stud in North Wales), *Skye* (home now after several years in Holland), *Sheriff* (at Stud in Denmark), *Shane* (North Dakota, *USA*), *Skylark*, producing some lovely foals at home, and

Scarlet (Thelma Pritchard). *Sepia*'s son (by *Revel Hello*), *Gleinant Sinbad* is with the Darby's at the Temptye Stud in Kent. *Sinbad* does everything from siring lovely foals to winning countless championships both in-hand and in harness.

Amongst many other additions to the stud in 1993, Pauline and her daughter, Catherine Jones, acquired *Revel Sequoia* who was always a favourite of hers. The following year she produced *Gleinant Snaffles* who was the best colt foal that Pauline had ever seen. He has won at Lampeter, Youngstock Champion at Glanusk, has twice won the West Midland Stallion Show, Shropshire & West Midlands Male Champion and silver medal, Champion at Royal Cornwall, Youngstock Champion and Reserve Overall Champion A, Youngstock Champion and Champion Welsh Yearling at Severn Valley, has won the Royal Bath & West and was placed at the Royal Welsh Show twice. Shown for Gleinant as a yearling by David Duggan. *Snaffles* was also shown as a three and six year old by Richard Miller. As six year-old, *Snaffles* was broken to ride, and was ridden by two children after only a few days under saddle. Used very little until he was five years, he is producing wonderful quality foals who inherit his super conformation, natural movement and beautiful head.

Gleinant ponies have been sold to many countries abroad. The ponies are Hill Ponies, bred for type, then conformation with which the movement should come. The aim is for substance, good bone, feather, lovely heads, big, bold eyes, small ears, a dished face with small neat muzzles. Hardiness. The Gleinant ponies and those like them could still carry a man up the hill as they used to do a hundred years ago.

RHOSON

Rhoson Stud of Section B ponies was established officially with the WPCS in 1971 by John and Glenys Davies, with the foundation mare, *Claydon Blue Chip* (*Bluey*), a combination of Coed Coch and Weston bloodlines; *Bluey* was the one most important ingredient in the type of pony bred at Rhoson. Beautiful in every way, the epitomy of what a Welsh Pony should be, she was with the Stud until she sadly died at 24 years and is buried in view of the Preseli mountains. The next purchases in successive years were two foals, *Downland Baled* and *Downland Rhamant*: both have spent their days creating their own lineage in the progress of the stud. The first colt to run at Rhoson was *Cippyn Man O'war*, who came on holiday as a yearling and stayed to be the first stud stallion. He and *Bluey* cast the mould for the lovely Welsh heads, with perhaps a little help from *Lydstep Royalty* (x *Bluey*), via *Rhoson Awel Mai* who John rates as possibly the best and most prepotent mare that the Stud has bred. Sadly she was to pass away at the young age of seven leaving *Rhoson Mandinka* who later sired *Rhoson Taranaki*, who was to play an important part in the future development of the stud. The orphan foal at foot, *Rhoson Mirain*, became a show winner, being unbeaten as a foal and introducing the Davies' son, Meirion, to the delights of showing.

The Stud's next stallion was *Downland Rembrandt* and he proved to be a lovely stallion, a real gentleman and a super stock getter. The following stallion was bred by Meirion, out of *Downland Rosewood* which he bought from Mrs Ann Berryman. *Rhoson Gaugin*, a colt, was many times a Supreme Champion as a yearling. His greatest achievement, however, was to run with the mares at the Downland Stud, the only outside stallion to do so since at least the start of the seventies. The present Stud stallion is *Eyarth Harlequin,* the top sire in Holland for many years, who will share his duties with *Shem* and *Taranaki.*

Pennwood Santa Monica, which John purchased from the original dispersal sale of the Pennwood Stud, has made an indelible mark on the Rhoson Stud and her three sons reside in North America where they are making their mark at stud and in the show ring. More importantly, they and other stallions and mares of the Rhoson stock have brought the Stud many wonderful friends, all sharing the pleasure and privilege of owning and breeding Welsh Ponies.

To date the Rhoson Stud has bred six individual Royal Welsh first-prize winners and a winning progeny group – *Cadwgan, Hudol, Gaugin, Sipsi, Carel* and *Shem.*

The Rhoson ponies have given the Stud great pleasure, making them friends all over the world. But for all the showing days and sales, nothing rivals the delight of watching them, peacefully grazing at home at Rhoson.

PARC

The Parc Stud of Welsh Cobs and Section C ponies has been involved in breeding and showing for an uninterrupted span of 150 years, a record of which the present owners, S D Morgan and sons, Daniel, John and Richard, are justifiably proud, especially as their present stock are the direct descendants of the original bloodlines of the 1840s. Great-great-grandfather Samuel Davies was an inspection judge and one of the founder members of the Welsh Pony and Cob Society Stud Book at the turn of the century. At that time he registered the stock using the prefix 'Ormond', which is the name of the folley on the farm, and D O Morgan JP, perpetuated the interest in the Cobs and in 1935 he changed the prefix to 'Parc'.

Parc Welsh Maid was covered by *Matharafal* at the 1947 Royal Welsh Show at Carmarthen and the following year one of the most beautiful Cobs ever was born and registered – *Parc Lady*. During her illustrious showing career *Parc Lady* won the Prince of Wales Cup at the Royal Welsh Show on four consecutive occasions in 1958, '59, '60 and '61. The mating of *Pentre Eiddwen Comet* and *Parc Lady* produced *Parc Pride* and *Parc Welsh Flyer*, amongst the most noteworthy. *Parc Pride* herself produced many noteworthy Cobs, the most famous being *Parc Rachel* and *Parc Dafydd*, both by *Cahn Dafydd,* and *Parc Bonheddwr* by *Ceredigion Twysog. Parc Rachel* won the Prince of Wales Cup, the supreme accolade for Welsh Cobs, in 1971, '72 and '75.

The most influential Parc Mare is *Parc Angharad* out of *Parc Rachel* by *Parc Bonheddwr*. She produced *Parc Gwenllian* and *Parc Alice*, who is now with Preben Russell, who also has *Parc Maggie May*, and *Parc Reveller*, now moved to Wales from Denmark. *Parc Angharad*'s grand-daughters are *Parc Eluned* and *Parc Medi*. Other exceptional mares perpetuating the bloodlines at Parc are *Parc Roslin*, out of *Parc Rachel*, and *Cathedine Margaret*, sired by *Parc Welsh Flyer*.

Stallions at Stud at Parc at present are *Parc Cardi* [1984, black, 14.2hh; sire: *Hewid Cardi*, dam: *Parc Rachel*]. *Parc Matador* [1988, dark bay, 14.2hh; sire: *Derwen Railway Express*, dam: *Parc Rachel*], and *Parc Welsh Dragon* [1992, chestnut, 14.1hh; sire: *Parc Welsh Flyer* dam: *Parc Roslin*]. *Parc Reveller*, initially leased by Preben Russell in Denmark, is now back in Wales, having been purchased by him.

Parc has been the home of the Section C breed certainly within living memory. The foundation mare *Parc Beauty* produced very good stock when mated with *Tanyffynnon Trustee*. One of her daughters, *Parc Black Beauty*, became an influential mare at the stud producing *Parc Annabell* by *Menai Fury* and *Parc Model* by *Synod William*. Show mare *Parc Ruby* is by *Synod Roger* and out of *Parc Annabell* and both *Parc Model* and *Parc Ruby* are proving

exceptional broodmares producing top quality stock. *Parc Model*'s daughters are *Parc Vanessa*, *Parc Maggie May* and *Parc Hazel*, who was Champion foal at the 1996 NPS at Malvern.

The aim at Parc is to breed quality animals of true Welsh characteristics from proven, successful female lines, of uninterrupted direct type. Parc is delighted to hear that Parc ponies and cobs provide their owners with success and pleasure both at home and overseas and a Welsh welcome awaits all visitors to the stud.

MINYFFORDD

Before Milton and Anna Jones had registered Welsh Cobs at Minyffordd they had Part-Breds for many years but, after going to the Royal Welsh Show around 1974 and seeing some of the Welsh Cobs mares there, they got bitten by the bug. The success of the Minyffordd Stud can be attributed to the emphasis placed on purchasing quality mares from established bloodlines, and the careful selection of stallions to suit these mares. Milton first bought a filly from the Nebo Stud and then a few years later purchased *Felinmor Miss Magic* at the Llanarth Sale from Keith Spenser. Since 1997 the Stud has shown the colt *Minyffordd Masterpiece*, who is line bred to *Nebo Black Magic*, and who won the two year-old colt class at the 1999 Royal Welsh Show. Milton covered five mares with him in 1999 and 2000. Five filly foals were born, one already sold to North Dakota in the USA where she has joined a long line of Minyffordd Cobs in the States and Canada including *Minyffordd Monteray*, *Minyffordd Maid Margaret* and *Minyffordd Desert Rose*. Also in 1999, through their export agency, Minyffordd helped in the export of *Telynau Royal Charter* to Tammy Burgin in California. This was the first Section B for Milton and Anna to export and he is making a name for himself out there.

Minyffordd Maid of Honour won the Cob Championship at the American Nationals and was Overall Champion in 1998 thereby providing two of *Dairy Maid*'s offspring to win the supreme American Championship, the other being *Minyffordd Megastar*. This, along with three Royal Welsh winners, *Marion*, *Megastar* and *Masterpiece*, makes *Dairy Maid* quite unique. She was also Reserve Female Champion herself in 1995.

In 2000 *Beech Hay Dairy Maid* produced a bay filly by *Pentrefelin Taliesin* and her daughter, *Maid Marion*, had a bay filly by *Masterpiece*. *Marion*'s daughter, *Mississipi Maid*, produced a black filly by *Masterpiece*, making four generations of the female line at Minyffordd. *Masterpiece* was sold in 2000, but not before he covered four of the best mares at Minyffordd who now have five bay mares at the Stud, three of them being first-prize winners at the Royal Welsh and the other two gaining second.

The aim of the stud is to continue to breed Cobs of true type and action, and as the Stud now has its full quota of mares and showing has decreased, future foals will be for sale.

TYMOR

Patsy Gibbons started Tymor Stud in 1987. Her first Welsh Cob purchase was the filly foal, *Cotleigh Rebecca,* x *Llanarth Flying Rocket*. *Rebecca*, who was Youngstock Champion at Northleach Show as a three year-old, produced a filly, *Tymor Temptress*, x *Crugybar Mabon Mai* [*Derwen Desert Express* x *Penardd Boremai*]. Also in 1987 Patsy acquired *Peris Heti*, who is by *Penllwynuchel Taran*, out of a *Nebo Daniel* mare. *Heti* has been a Supreme Champion many times and Scott, Patsy's son, won his first championship with her.

Derwen Germane [*Derwen Replica* x *Tireinon Gwenlas*], joined the stud in 1988. She was shown as a yearling and placed at both Lampeter Stallion show and the Royal Welsh as a yearling and was placed second in the International Broodmare class at Peterborough at only four years of age.

Due to Patsy and Scott's love of *Peris Heti*, the stud purchased the colt foal *Crugybar Mabon Mai* [*Derwen Desert Express* x *Pennardd Boremai*], who is half brother to *Pennllwynuchel Taran*. Through *Mabon* the stud produces the movement which comes from *Boremai* alone, as all *Mabon*'s sons and daughters have strong, forceful movement and cover the ground with great strength, the fillies being equal to the colts. *Mabon Mai* was sixth in the Sire Ratings, achieving this from only five animals shown and, considering that he is not at public stud, is a top stock getter. Both Patsy and Scott agree that before purchasing *Mabon* they bred nice foals from a lot of different stallions, but they were not of the class they are producing now with *Mabon*.

All the mares are of different types at Tymor, but all have produced superb, prizewinning stock by *Mabon*. *Derwen Germane* produced *Tymor Lamtara*. *Tardebigge Dawn Chorus* is the dam of *Tymor the Tramp*. The stocky little Cob mare, *Maesyrafon Cameo*, is the mother of *Tymor Pele*.

Also at the stud is *Crugybar Marged Mai*, a full sister to *Mabon*, who produced her first foal in 2000 by *Blaengwen Brenin*, a colt, who is a typical Tymor.

Patsy and Scott both say they thank their lucky stars that Tymor owns *Mabon Mai*, as they do not think they would have ever won at the Royal Welsh show without him.

CHAPTER NINE
STUDS ACROSS THE WORLD

DOORNZICHT STUD
HOLLAND

Benno and Claudia Crezee own the Doornzicht Stud of Welsh Mountain Ponies which began when they purchased their first pony in 1965, *Corndu Topsy, [Fayre Romeo x Corndu Trixie]*, using a stallion, *Triley Daylight*, the Stud bred a filly, *Dijkstra Evelien*, which was only registered with the *Dutch Stamboek*. *Evelien* produced nineteen foals for the Stud which have all been sold, and she became the foundation mare for the Stud. From 1966 to the present the Stud has bred over sixty foals in total, some of which have been kept on.

In 1983 Benno and Claudia bred a filly out of *Dijkstra Evelien* named *Doornzicht Emma* x *Blaenau Polish*. She was shown at the International Show when it was held in Ermelo and came third in the yearling class. Not shown a lot she is usually in the ribbons. In 1988 *Emma* produced a filly by *Wharley Symbol*, *Doornzicht Enid*, and as a foal she was shown with *Emma* at the International Show when it was held in Brussels, both coming third in their class. In 1995 *Emma* produced *Doornzicht Elena*, by *Foxhunter Pantheon [Penual Mark x Foxhunter Parakeet]*. *Doornzicht Elisan* is also out of *Emma* and was born

in 1996, by a Dutch bred stallion, *Bolster Goldleaf [Foxhunter Pantheon x Gemstone Golden Glory]*.

During 1993 Benno went to Wales to buy *Tiffwyl Music [Revel Humming Top x Tiffwyl Myfi x Clan Pip]*. *Music* stayed for some time in the UK to be covered by *Springbourne Caraway*. She produced a colt which Benno had hoped for, *Doornzicht Mozart*; however, the Stud was unlucky as he proved to be infertile. *Music* produced *Doornzicht Mazurka* in 1996, x *Foxhunter Pantheon*, who is still with the Stud.

Welsh Mountain Ponies have given Benno and Claudia a lot of pleasure so far and they hope to show many more homebred Doornzicht ponies.

DEROKS WELSH PONY AND COB STUD
GERMANY

Deroks Welsh Pony and Cob Stud began in November 1987 when the first mare, *Ionos Fancy [Parc Welsh Flyer x Ionos Dainty]*, laid the foundation for the stud. In the spring of 1988 the filly, *Deroks Dereclair*, the first foal, was born. Within the same year *Florida Star [Parc Welsh Flyer x Penlannoeth Sal]* joined the stud and also the stallion, *Greenway Double Diamond [Nebo Daniel x Arthen Aloma]*, an old-fashioned stallion with a lovely temperament, to cover the mares. The prefix Deroks was then registered taken from the initials of the founders, DETlev and Rolf KriSten.

At the Benelux Championships in 1989 they saw *Nebo Celebration* and in November 1989 they purchased *Ruska Affection [Nebo Celebration x Ruska Gwen]*, as a two year-old from Henk W. Van Dijk and Judith Alberts from whom they also purchased *Ruska Perl [Nebo Sportsman x Ruska Gwen]*, whose showing career began as a three year-old at the German Bundesschau in Standenbuhl (Pfalz) where *Perl* became Champion Section D, also in Wermelskirchen at the Rheinland Show the judges made her Overall Supreme Champion. After a foaling break in 1994, she was again twice Champion in 1995 and 1996, and also in 2000 she was Overall Supreme winner of the Rheinland Show. Perl also won the Belgian and Dutch Championships of 1998 in Putte, Belgium and Arcen, Netherlands. At the highly regarded German Bundesschau she left the show ring as Overall Supreme Champion, and in 2000 as Reserve Overall Supreme Champion, an impressive list of winnings.

The home bred *Deroks Welsh Model [Thorneyside Spring Magic x Ruska Affection]*, was only shown as a two year-old and that one year of 1997 she won three Reserve and Overall Section D Championships in Holland and Belgium.

Last, but by no means least, the smallest member of the Stud is *Deroks Lady Janet [Tyngwndwn Joker x Talon Lorna]*, Section C, born 1996. This Section C has also achieved a successful showing career being three times Reserve Overall Champion at the shows for Rheinland and two other contests in the Netherlands. In 2000 she received the Reserve Champion Section C title at the International Show in Holland. The Deroks Welsh Breeding has proved itself in the show ring many times over the years.

EKBACKEN WELSH MOUNTAIN PONY STUD
SWEDEN

Ekbacken Stud is owned by Inger Becker and her son Johan. She and her husband. Gosta, who sadly passed away in 1998, bought their first Welsh Mountain Pony in 1972. One day when visiting a horse dealer they saw a three year-old, dark chestnut mare, heavily in foal, which is unusual for three year-olds in Sweden, fell in love with her and bought her: *Egetofte Sunflower, x Belvoir Dandelion [Revel Favour x Belvoir Daffodil] x Gwyndyucha Shan [Rhyd-y-Felin Sherry x Aled Gwyneth]*. Two weeks later *Sunflower* produced a fabulous colt, *Ekbackens Moonbeam, x Twyford Tomboy*. He was a dark chestnut with a blaze and four white socks. When *Moonbeam* was three he got his stallion licence and now the Stud had a stallion and no mares to breed from. Inger and Gosta then bought three mares from the Egetofte Stud in Denmark, *Egetofte Bettina [Coed Coch Asa x Gurnos Beth], Revel Tassie [Clan*

Tony x *Mountain Tess]*, and *Ceulan Madam Butterfly [Pendock Puccini x Gwen Tafarn Gem]*. *Madam Butterfly* had arrived at Egetofte as a six year-old with a colt foal, *Gredington Bugail*, at foot who became one of the most influential stallions in Denmark and was the Supreme Champion at the National Danish Show seven times in a row. They covered *Madam Butterfly* with *Ekbackens Moonbeam* and she produced a colt, *Ekbackens Krumelur*, who has been a very good stockgetter and has won many Championships in the show ring. *Madam Butterfly* produced two more colts and then her only filly foal with the Stud, *Ekbackens Butterfly,* who became a Diploma mare. Diplomas are given to the best three year-old fillies in Sweden, and she in turn produced Diploma fillies.

In 1978 *Gredington Juliet [Dinas Nwfus x Gredington Dwyfol]*, was purchased from England, also *Twyford Seed [Rowfant Sepoy x Twyford Sunflower]*, who had a colt foal at foot and was in foal to *Twyford Gamecock*. The true success of the Stud is due to Twyford Seed together with the Ekbacken stallions. *Twyford Seed* with *Moonbeam* produced some lovely daughters, *Ekbackens Black Jolly, Ekbackens Cinderella* and *Ekbackens Sofia. Sofia,* a Diploma mare, produced *Ekbackens Signal* who has won Championships both in Dressage and Show Jumping. In 1985 *Moonbeam* sadly died, aged thirteen years, so Inger and Gosta visited Twyford Stud and purchased *Twyford My Man*, from Mrs Alison Mountain. *My Man* has been an asset to the Stud and at the latest Grading Show he was rewarded with ELIT and is now the only living Welsh Mountain stallion with ELIT. *My Man* is now eighteen years-old and has produced several daughters for which the Stud needed a stallion. In the summer of 2000 they bought a yearling colt from the Heniarth Stud in Wales. He is *Heniarth Mr Milligan [Roseisle Pandy Tudor x Sunwillow Mutters]*, and he won his class at the Royal Welsh Show a few days afterwards.

THE RIBBLE VALLEY PONY STUD ALICANTE, SPAIN

Sue Horey had a love affair with Welsh Ponies for years and in 1996, with the encouragement of her husband, Paul, she decided to start breeding Welsh Ponies again, but in Spain where they now lived. Sue travelled to Wales, where she bought a stallion, *Cadlan Valley Gamestar*, a colt, *Nefydd Bucaneer*, a filly, *Eyarth Zircon*, and two in-foal mares, *Hilin Siriol* and *Mybella Belinda*, which were all exported to Spain in 1997. They eventually arrived in Spain to temperatures in the 80s, but quickly became acclimatised.

Setting up the stud in Spain has been great fun, but not without its hiccups. These were soon overcome and did not dampen Sue and Paul's spirits. Sue experienced a rude awakening during those first months, however, having to forget how she kept the ponies in England and learn a whole new regime. There is no grazing in that part of Spain so the ponies have to be fed between three and five times a day, and the Horey's emulate grazing as much as they can by scattering Alfalfa and eating straw over the paddocks, therefore making the ponies work for their food. They get two hard feeds a day, alfalfa three times a day and Sue buys 100 kilos of carrots a week, ensuring that they have something succulent to eat each day. Sue also buys fruits in season at reduced prices and the ponies love them. In late winter and early spring they cut their crop of vetch and oats, which they feed as a green crop. This is good because it is 'cut and grow again' and the eating programme which Sue and Paul have devised keeps the ponies occupied naturally without risking laminitis or other feed-related diseases.

With virtually no grazing, Sue's main concern for the ponies was boredom, and the ponies are therefore kept amused with various toys and training sessions. Coping with the high temperatures caused further initial concern. The mares and foals are kept in at night and during the hottest part of the day, as are the two entires. The yearlings are out night and day but have an enormous field shelter, which is kept bedded down and provides shelter from the sun. Sue says it is much harder work keeping ponies there, but even that has it's positive side, as all the ponies are handled so much more and the foals learn all their lessons very early.

The general response to the ponies has been excellent, and Sue and Paul intend starting a Pony Club to teach the children there not only how to ride but how to look after and care for ponies. Sue is working hard for the Welsh Breeds in Spain and has helped to translate the Welsh Pony and Cob Society's promotional Breeds leaflet into Spanish in order that the people in Spain can learn about the Welsh Breeds.

RUSKA WELSH COB STUD HOLLAND

The Ruska Welsh Cob Stud is owned by Henk van Dijk and Judith Alberts and was founded in 1972. The first mare Henk bought was the 15hh dun mare, *Sawel Aures [Llanarth Braint* x *Hercws Victory Pride]*. The first round of many stud visits was made around Lampeter Stallion Show 1973. Their first visit to Nebo Stud was decisive for their choice for Welsh Type, movement and character. In 1973 they visited studs around Lampeter Stallion Show and Nebo Stud had the Welsh type, movement and character that they liked. The Stud's first stallion was the typey, compact, 14.2hh, bay, *Nebo Comet [Parc Welsh Flyer* x *Nebo Beauty]* sweet-natured and a good mover he won Stallion classes and threw very nice foals for the Stud.

After almost nine years of farming sheep and beef in Wales, Henk returned to Holland taking with him *Ruska Gwen* and her daughter *Ruska*

Rowena, and joined partners with Hans Strelin. First Henk leased *Nebo Celebration [Nebo Daniel* x *Tyngwndwn Mathrafal Lady]*, as a young stallion. He won the Dutch Young Stallion Class, was Overall Supreme Champion at Aachen and left some top mares. Later Nebo bought him back and he is now in Denmark. He then bought the stallion, *Nebo Sportsman [Nebo Brenin* x *Tyngwndwn Mathrafal Lady]* for driving and covering mares. *Degla Country Flyer [Parc Welsh Flyer* x *Degla Country Rose]*, and *Thorneyside Spring Magic [Brynymor Welsh Magic* x *Thorneyside Melody]* were bought later for the same purpose; they both won many first prizes and Championships In-Hand also.

Then the Stud decided to breed Section Cs and Henk purchased the promising yearling, *Felinmor Dymunol [Nebo Brenin* x *Stremda Jet]*, in the sales. *Tyngwyndwn Joker* sired two of her foals, and *Tyngwyndwn Master*, one, then they purchased a stallion, the top sire in Denmark, *Synod Grouse [Synod Roger* x *Synod Gem]*. They also purchased *Tremymor Sir Geraint* in 1999 *[Nebo Brenin* x *Tremymor Swynol]*. Eventually the Stud purchased quite a few mares, selected on breeding, type and capability to perform. First was the black mare, *Tewgoed Magic Lady [Nebo Black Magic* x *Hewid Nest]*, she was driven in harness and produced the Stud's first two stallions. Hans Strelin also bought her granddaughter, *Tewgoed Rosebud [Nebo Brenin* x *Tewgoed Mari]* as a foal. Together with *Northleach*

Duchess, she was top of the Youngstock classes for several years, crowning her achievements with the Youngstock Championship at Brussels International Show. She was twice Dutch National Champion Mare, the only times shown in Holland, and proved to be a very good breeder.

Many more Cobs and Section Cs have been bred and passed through the hands of Ruska Stud over the years, many have won prizes, and some have performed in harness. As the Stud has a limited amount of land they now keep nine mares and sell most of the foals and youngsters on, covering roughly half the mares each year.

The diversity of the Welsh Breeds, the hardiness and above all the temperament, suits the Ruska Stud who consider the Welsh Cob to be very useful in a broad range of equine sports compared to other breeds. The Ruska Stud breeds foals that are a credit to their Welsh Breed in every way.

THE ZONNEWEIDE STUD HOLLAND

The Zonneweide Stud was started in 1979 by Arjan de Rade, together with his father. His mother chose the prefix for the stud, which means 'Sunny Field'. The first pony at the Stud, *Bleekwaard Renske*, x *Twyford Mystic*, was purchased from one of the earliest Dutch Welsh Mountain pony breeders, Mrs Snoek – v.d. Hoeven.

Renske was covered by *Coed Coch Brodor* and

produced the first filly of the stud and another daughter of this famous stallion on Holland came to the stud. The first stud stallion at Zonneweide was *Blaenau Chelsea Fan* which Arjan purchased from Mr Boumans from Deurne, who encouraged young Arjan as it was unusual at this time to keep your own stallion in Holland. Most of the breeders were making use of the service of the stallion keepers and most of them were faithful to one stallion keeper.

The de Rade family purchased *Fuchsia (H) Ilona [Bengad Cockles* x *Fuchsia Pollyanna],* as a foal and the enthusiasm of the family knew no bounds as this filly was a great mover and a winner in the show ring, also proving herself to be an excellent broodmare. It was because of *Ilona* that her full sister, her dam, *Grada*, and much later, as an eighteen year-old, *Grada*'s half sister, were also purchased. The descendants of this line were also kept to set up a main family of the Zonneweide ponies.

As a first ridden pony for Arjan's little sister, *Menai Sandy* came to the stud as well. Besides her work at the Pony Club, she also produced foals, mostly colts. *Sandy* was not a regular breeder, but one of the colts was very special to Arjan and became also of great importance to the stud, *Zonneweide Hamid*, x *Carolinas Moonshine*, a grandson of *Coed Coch Madog. Zonneweide Hamid* suited *Fuchsia Illona* very well and they had seven foals together, each of them being a very good mover.

Ilona was a rather fine-boned mare and therefore another important purchase was made, the big, and exceptional mover *Springbourne Hazel,* x *Penual Mark,* and her foal, *Vechtzicht's Heather,* x *Vechtzicht's Harmony*, came to the stud. It was Arjan's plan that besides being the true-to-type Welsh Mountain ponies, the Zonneweide ponies should have scope and movement as well.

It was this task and the ponies themselves that were left when, Arjan only twenty nine years-old, died suddenly, after showing one of his ponies at a show. His wife, Janneke de Rade – Teeuwen, was the person of the de Rade family who kept most of the ponies and wanted to continue the stud, the ponies proving to be a great comfort to Janneke after the loss of her beloved husband. The Zonneweide ponies still keep the memory of the stud's founder alive.

After Arjan's death a lot of plans and dreams came true. *Zonneweide Hamid* became Supreme Champion at a show with British judges. Two of the mares were sent to England to be covered by *Springbourne Caraway*, producing two colt foals the following year, of which *Jacinto* was retained. 1985 was the first time that a pony for the Stud was purchased in Wales, which was the filly foal, *Bwlch-y-Gwynt Caryl [Nerwyn Cadno* x *Verdrefawr Blodwen]. Zonneweide Nico* became approved stallion at the very strict Dutch Stallion Show in February 1996. *Zonneweide Norelja*, x *Boreas Ilias*, became Best

Dutch three year-old at the National Mare Show in 1996. *Vechtzicht's Heather* has been Champion as well and also produced the spectacularly moving and successful show filly, *Zonneweide Heidie,* x *Zonneweide Nico. Bwlch-y-Gwynt Caryl* became a very beautiful show pony, being National Youngstock Champion and, as a five year-old, it is hoped she will have a great show career in front of her. *Zonneweide Iron Lady,* x *Iange Voren Napels,* became Best Dutch Three Year-Old in 1999, and *Zonneweide Prinses* produced for her new owner *Vennebos Summer Fun,* x *Lange Voren Charles,* who became Best Approved Stallion and was a Medal winner at the Stallion Show of 2000.

Janneke in the meantime married again and is now living with her husband, Egbert-Jan Schilthuis. The Zonneweide Stud joined the Windhoek Welsh Mountain Pony Stud in the very north-eastern part of Holland called Groningen. Both studs kept to their own policies although they have a few important things in common. The stud stallions are now the fifteen year-old *Zonneweide Hamid, Zonneweide Jacinto* and *Zonneweide Juppie.* To add fresh blood and improve type at the stud, *Vechtzicht's Comet,* x *Springbourne Claret,* was recently purchased. The colt, *Lustcord Beauty,* x *Ceulan Cariadog* and out of a Zonneweide mare, is there as a future stallion. With the old, *fantastic Fuchsia (H)* broodmares still going, nice young mares to be shown and the new bloodlines of the stallions, the Zonneweide Stud is still very much alive and hopes to continue the hobby for many years.

CHAPTER TEN

PERFORMANCE PONIES
SECTIONS A AND B

BALEDON

The Baledon Stud was formed in approximately 1960 after the owner, Miss Ann Bale-Williams, had a serious riding accident and was advised not to ride again. Welsh Mountain ponies seemed to fit the bill as she would not be tempted to ride them, they being too small but being ideal children's ponies, so Miss Bale-Williams could still derive pleasure from breeding, breaking and schooling them and turn out the finished article under saddle.

Baledon Rhianfa was the first to be broken to ride in 1965 and she had a season under saddle before becoming a brood mare and, being a success, she laid the foundation for all the Baledon ponies. *Baledon May Lady* was broken to ride, her first jockey being Mrs K. Cuff's grandson Timothy Rees, and she then went on to Polly Lyons, the three-day event rider. Over the years this pony has been loaned to many families and at thirty years old she still belongs to the stud. *Baledon Sunbeam* and *Baledon Mercutio* were both placed at the Royal Welsh in the Leading Rein classes. *Baledon Chief* was the stud's first Section B to come out under saddle before he was sold. *Baledon Nobleman* was sold to New York and was ridden by the owner's daughter until she grew out of him, then he was used in harness.

By far the most famous ridden Baledon pony was *Commanchero* who won well over 200 Championships in Mountain and Moorland, Ridden Showing and Working Hunter Pony classes. He is one of the few Native ponies to qualify for Olympia eight times, a feat for which the Stud was presented with the Broderick Trophy. The amount of publicity he brought the Welsh Section Bs was phenomenal, bringing to the fore how versatile the breed could be. At that time there were not so many Section Bs competing under saddle and the tremendous boom in the ridden Section Bs is thanks mainly due to people seeing *Commanchero* under saddle. He was so versatile, he was an outstanding jumper, qualifying for the finals at the NPS and then for the Horse of the Year Show. In the early days of the NPS Working Hunter Pony Finals, the larger Section Bs over 13hh had to jump in the 14.2hh class with the Large Breeds which included

Section D, New Forest and Connemaras etc. He was five inches smaller than the big 14.2hh but still managed to get round the course, ending up third and fourth in the two years before the rules were changed.

Baledon dams were also responsible for the two other Olympia finalists. *Baledon Rose Queen* was the dam of *Skellorn Rose Princess* who qualified three times and *Baledon Country Girl* was the dam of *Eden Tree Country Vogue* who qualified twice.

Baledon Section Bs have always been the well-up-to-height riding type with tremendous movements which has always made them an ideal riding pony for children or small adults.

FFRETHI

At Ffrethi Stud, owned and run by Katy Girdler, the emphasis is on producing Native Ponies to be shown under saddle. Katy prefers to show stallions, although finding the right ponies is very difficult as only a few stallions ever make top ridden ponies. They have to show all the presence of a stallion, but with the manners of a gelding and there are not many ponies around which fit this criterion, which is why the stud does not mix breeding with showing, as any lapse in manners is a problem. Only in ridden Native Pony classes are stallions ridden with mares and geldings and they must behave impeccably.

Among the stud's top Welsh Ponies is *Menai Furious [Menai Fury x Meiarth Blodwen]*, bred by

Peter and Ann Jones of the Menai Stud in 1982. *Furious* came to Ffrethi in the Autumn of 1990 to be produced for the 1991 season, He stayed, and now, aged nineteen years, he is a permanent resident at the stud. In an amazing show career Katy and *Furious* twice won the Supreme Ridden Championship for Welsh Cobs at the Royal Welsh Show in 1993 and 1994, and also Championships at the National Pony Society and Ponies UK Championship shows. He represented the WPCS at various displays, including the National Pony Society Centenary and the WPCS International Show. A prolific winner, he has won the National Points for Section C stallions every year that he has competed. In 1999 he came out of retirement to take up Dressage and in 2000 he won the Millennium Dressage Challenge at Ponies UK Championships; he also enjoyed another WPCS display at the Ceredigion Area Centenary in Talsarn in the same year.

Priestwood Valentino [Weston Regent x Breccles Showgirl], is a Welsh Section B stallion, born in 1991, bred by Gillian and David Sells and bought by Ffrethi as a weaned foal from Fayre Oaks sale. He had many successes as a youngster, in-hand, including winning at Lampeter Stallion show as a yearling. By the time he came out ridden as a four year-old he was quite used to the show ring and immediately began to win the big shows, Royal Bath and West, Devon County, Royal of England, Champion Royal Welsh, National Pony Society and Ponies UK Performance Champion. In 1996 he became the National Pony Society Novice Pony of the Year and in four years' top level showing has the almost unbelievable total of wins at sixty two shows of sixty nine class wins and forty one Championships. He was also shown in-hand during these years and won the A & B Section of the Glyn Greenwood Native Pony In-Hand Championship.

OVINGTON

Ovington Stud, was started by Mrs Patricia Corbett and a friend, Mrs Henry Bruce; they purchased three Stoatley mares from Miss A. Muir, one Section B and two Section As and a short while later, a Coed Coch mare was purchased from Miss Broderick. Mrs Corbett was bitten by the showing bug and as Mrs Bruce did not want to show, Mrs Corbett continued the Stud on her own.

Realising that she had not got the type of ponies that she really liked, ones with extravagant movement, quality and presence, Mrs Corbett contacted Miss Broderick at the Coed Coch Stud, but unfortunately she had nothing of the type that Mrs Corbett wanted at a suitable price and suggested that she should try Mr Owen Ellis of the Hendre Stud. So in the autumn of 1961, together with Miss Gillian Coleman, they stood on a hill in a thunderstorm watching a herd of ponies driven past. Mrs Corbett became the owner of *Hendre Blodwen V1 [Hendre Hawddgai* x *Hendre Blodwen 11* x *Tan-y-Bwlch Berwyn]* and she became the foundation mare

of the Ovington Stud. *Blodwen* was in foal to *Coed Coch St. Iwan [Coed Coch Madog* x *Coed Coch Siaradus]* and produced *Ovington Athena* who was all that a delighted Mrs Corbett had hoped for, as besides being good-looking she was a natural to show. *Hendre Blodwen* and *Ovington Athena* both won at Northleach, two of *Blodwen*'s progeny also did very well, *Ovington Cassandra* also winning at Northleach when owned by Mr and Mrs Curtis of the Kingsmead Stud. Ridden by Miss Curtis, *Ovington Desdemona* also won a lot under saddle, as did her daughter, *Ovington Isis*, x *Treharne Tomboy*. She began her career by winning at the South of England as a yearling. Mrs Corbett was very fortunate to have Fiona and Sara Baigent to ride and show the ponies for her. *Isis* did very well in the Leading Rein and First Ridden classes, then she started jumping, also being shown as a brood mare in 1978, she won the Mountain and Moorland Championship at Alresford Show.

Ovington Hercules was a lovely golden dun gelding, a prolific winner for Mrs Gay Turvill with her daughter Joanna; he then went on to have many wins for the author, ridden by her son, Julian Bell-Mckenna, in the Leading Rein classes during 1975-6 coming second out of twenty eight forward at the Aldershot County Show under Dame Sybil Smith. *Ovington Desdemona* was another prolific winner under saddle.

During 1970 a son of *Hendre Blodwen*, *Ovington Sir Galahad*, x *Furnace Landlord*, when a yearling, jumped two lots of posts and rails into the mare's paddock. All the mares being safely in foal Mrs Corbett thought nothing of this until *Blodwen* did not foal to her dates but in the autumn produced a filly, *Ovington Idyll*, by her son. Many of *Idyll's* progeny, who have a double line back to *Blodwen*, have been a great help to the stud, either doing well being shown or breeding winners. A son, *Ovington Remus*, x *Bengad Nepeta*, stood at the Forlan Stud, siring some good stock before being sold to Denmark where he has been first in the sire ratings for the Section As.

Ovington Pandora, x *Bengad Nepeta*, is the dam of *Ovington Xandu*, x *Springbourne Herian*. Mrs Corbett knew he was special from the day he was born and he did very well for her before he was sold to Miss Vanessa Neal in whose ownership he has continued to make his mark. A very versatile pony, he won In-Hand, Under Saddle and now is a winner In Harness.

Over the years Mrs. Corbett has bought various ponies but has found that the ones she kept were always descendants of *Hendre Blodwen VI* and every year there is the excitement of hoping for another *Athena*.

ROWFANTINA

The well-known Rowfantina Stud of Welsh Mountain Ponies owned by Mrs Jean Shemilt and Mrs Mandy Burchall-Small have proved to be exceptional children's ponies by their prolific winnings in the show ring, and not only does Mandy Burchall-Small breed ponies, she also buys in what she considers to be suitable future ridden show ponies, and produces them in the show ring with phenomenal success.

Most probably one of the best-known and most successful of the Rowfantina ponies is the lovely grey mare, *Rowfantina Old Fashioned [Coed Coch Pernod, Rowfantina Onette]*. She was bred in the USA by Mandy's mother, Mrs Jean Shemilt, who returned to England from the States bringing with her *Rowfantina Old Fashioned* and the then twenty year-old *Coed Coch Pernod*. Mandy herself broke in *Old Fashioned*, 10 years old, and by January 1999 she had already been placed Champion Under Saddle. During the 1999 season *Old Fashioned* won approximately thirty first prizes, sixteen Championships and three Supreme Championships, including the Spring Ardingly, Royal Windsor, the South of England and the Lobsterpot at the PUK Summer Championships; she also qualified for the HOYS. During 2000 she again won at the Spring Ardingly and was Champion, repeating her win again at Royal Windsor. She qualified for HOYS at Newmarket and was Reserve Champion in the Lead Rein final at the NPS Summer Championships, having won the Open Lead Rein Qualifier at the NPS the day before. Finally she won and was also Champion at Wembley HOYS. Beautifully ridden throughout the two years by Mandy's seven year-old son, Owen Small,

Rowfantina Old Fashioned is now retired from her riding career to breed and show In-Hand.

Rowfantina Nureyev was a Part-Bred Palomino gelding, standing approximately 11.2hh. He began his career with a win and never looked back! While owned by Mandy he won the Novice Lead Rein Final at the PUK and qualified for the Royal International, where he was fifth, and also qualified for Wembley where he was seventh. He was then sold to the Roles family where he went on to win nearly every County Show in the Country, his main wins being the Royal Welsh, the Royal, the Royal International and the Championship in 1995 and a second at the HOYS and Reserve Champion in 1995. He was second at the HOYS in 1997 and died on November 5th, 1997, of colic – a terrible shame.

On a visit to Wales during 1993 Mandy came across a two year-old Palomino colt which she liked the look of, so bought him and took him home to England. This colt was *Cwmbachstel Dion*, bred by John and Brenda Williams of Crugybar Stud, and as they were not keeping him they registered him with their second prefix, *Cwmbachstel*, selling him as a foal. *Dion* is out of *Penllyn Scylla*, who was on permanent lease to Crugybar Stud, and by *Penllyn Meurig*.

Dion was used at stud both by Mandy and on lease to Rosemary Phillipson-Stowe of the Pendock Stud. *Rowfantina Peter Pan*, a gelding by *Dion* and out of *Lacey Prima*, has recently been sold to a showing family and *Rowfantina Rosalind*, a chestnut filly, by *Dion*, out of *Weston Rosette*, will be retained permanently by the stud.

Dion's riding career began in 1999 when he qualified for the PUK Winter Championships and won at several winter shows. He then won the Novice Mountain and Moorland WHP at PUK Winter Championships and went on to be Champion. This put him through to the Champion of Champions. He then went on to win the Novice Mountain and Moorland Working Hunter Pony final at Malvern, the NPS Summer Show, and at the PUK Summer Championships. All three major Novice Working Hunter Pony Championships were won by him. He was first and Reserve Champion at Essex County in the Olympia Qualifier. He qualified for HOYS at the East Anglia Native Show and of course went on to win the final and the Championship. He was Reserve Supreme Points Winner at the end of the season. The above are only just a few of his results! He was sold to the Bright family in late 1999 for Robert to show.

SIANWOOD

John James took over ownership of the Sianwood Stud in the mid seventies following the death of Mr Jo Baker-Jones of the Cambrian Recording Company. Prior to this John had managed the Stud for him and his wife Doreen, and enjoyed much success with Section Bs and in-hand riding ponies.

Sianwood Jazmyn is one which the stud still has today. She won the Royal of England in 1975 and later as a brood mare at the Royal Welsh. She is also the dam of the Wembley ponies, *Sianwood Footprint* and *Sianwood Honeycomb*. In 1981 John gained the valuable assistance of Ann on a permanent basis when she became his wife and it was from then on that the stud's momentum increased. They were very fortunate to acquire *Cennen Galena* in the mid eighties from Mr and Mrs Emrys Bowen of the Cennen Stud. *Galena* already had a big reputation, having been Champion of the Royal of England and also British Mountain and Moorland In-Hand Champion. It is safe to say that *Galena* founded the Section B ponies which Sianwood has today. Her first foal was *Sianwood Goldrush*, currently the stud's senior stallion and the sire of many, many winners at home and abroad. Her second foal, a full brother to *Downland Kruggerand*, was *Silvermine* and his is a story on its own.

Sianwood Silvermine was born a chestnut in 1988 and turned grey whilst on his return to Downland with his mother late that summer. John showed him lightly as a yearling and advertised him at stud as a two year-old by which time he had turned iron grey, perhaps not the most fashionable of colours but nonetheless a beautifully-made pony, a particularly good mover with a tremendous walk. However, potential customers were put off by the colour, as chestnuts, bays and browns were more in vogue. Nevertheless John used *Silvermine* and one of his progeny stands at the world famous Langtree Stud of Jan Langley near Melbourne, Australia. He is called *Silversmith* and is out of *Aberchrychan Antonia* who had joined Sianwood when Mrs Thomas retired. By this time David James, John and Ann's son, had started riding. He is the same age as *Silvermine*, and was having great fun on a little Welsh pony called *Pippin* which John had bought from Hereford market. Tragically *Pippin* died of Cushing's disease. David was offered another pony and of course, it had to be another grey. By now *Silvermine* was beginning to look to be an excellent stock getter, as *Galena* had produced yet another super colt, a chestnut, by *Downland Arcady*, called *Sianwood Arcade*, sire of *Cennen Seraphine*, Royal of England Champion, so *Silvermine* was offered to David. Philippa, David's older sister, nurtured *Silvo*, as he is affectionately known, through his novice term under saddle winning Ridden Section B and Mountain and Moorland First Ridden classes. During this period he was still being shown In-Hand, winning regularly at Northleach, Pembroke County, The Three Counties etc.; in fact, most shows for which he was entered. To date, the highlight of his showing career has been his winning the ridden Section B class at the Royal Welsh in 1999 and ultimately being Reserve Champion – a very, very proud day for those at Sianwood, having bred, schooled and produced both the pony and the rider.

TEIFI

Welsh Ponies and Cobs have been registered under the Teifi prefix since 1902 when the Welsh Pony and Cob Society decided to compile and publish stud books of our native breeds. Teifi stud is now owned by Stuart Lloyd and his partner, Dee. (See profile on pages 103-4).

Following the success achieved with the Welsh Cob Stallion *Dimbeth Sion,* Stuart and Dee bought a Section A mare, *Trefaes Perl*, a typical Welsh Mountain Pony mare that they showed in-hand and, as she was ten years when they bought her, they did not attempt to break her in to perform. However, in the autumn of 1998 Stuart and Dee decided to look for a Welsh Mountain Pony Stallion and after looking long and hard they went back to the Trefaes Stud and purchased *Trefaes Guardsman*. He was a six year-old who was running with a band of mares and had done so for the previous two years.

On arriving at his new home, he was given time to settle into his surroundings. He was wormed, shod and received a visit from the dentist. He was exercised by walking out in-hand and also in the horsewalker. Tack was introduced gradually and he was mouthed carefully. He took everything in his stride. The first week in May saw him in a cart for the first time and he was showing that he had rare talent, so Stuart and Dee entered him for the Royal Welsh Show, his first outing for them. On the Tuesday morning he won his In-Hand class of Junior stallions from the 34 entries and on returning to the main ring on Wednesday captured the Male Championship of the breed, beating the senior stallion and Youngstock Champion in the process. On the Tuesday evening he competed in the Welsh Pony Harness Driving Class, his first ever show in harness, which was held in the vast arena in the main ring and in front of a daunting Grandstand. He did not put a hoof out of place, and it was a very closely-contested class with the first two ponies being asked for an extra run-out. He was placed second which was a magnificent achievement for a pony that had only some weeks previously been put into a cart for the very first time.

His sire is *Skellorn Daylight*, an extremely good stock getter that has won the progeny award at the Royal Welsh on numerous occasions. His dam is a proven brood mare of high repute that was also a very successful show mare, *Trefaes Grey Lady*, who was also a progeny award winner at the Royal Welsh Show.

Guardsman is a wonderful example of Stuart and Dee's experience with our native breed.

With *Dimbeth Sion* taking the showing world by storm (see pages 103-4), Stuart received an invitation to go and produce a Welsh Pony in the USA. The pony was to be shown in the All American National Welsh Show which was held as part of the State Fair, in Tulsa, Oklahoma.

Sleight of Hand, a Section B stallion, had a natural talent, very much in the same mould as *Sion*. He took the Supreme Champion Honours and went on to complete a treble as he was judged Supreme in the 1988, 1991 and 1997 American Nationals. The 1997 show was an historic event in that for the first time a Welsh Pony and Cob Society Medal, presented by the Parent Society of Wales, was given to the Supreme Champion. *Sleight* has now retired from the show ring after setting a record that will be difficult to emulate. He was produced and shown by Stuart on all three occasions.

Sleight is owned by Gail and Arthur Tomson of the Gayfields Stud, USA, who are regular visitors to Wales. His dam, *Coed Coch Olwen*, was bought at the final dispersal sale of the Coed Coch Stud, Abergele, in 1978, the same day that Lady Creswick of Australia set up a United Kingdom auction record when buying *Coed Coch Bari* for 21,000 guineas. *Sleight*'s sire is *Mylncroft Spun Gold*, a well-known sire of performance Champions.

CHAPTER ELEVEN

PERFORMANCE PONIES AND HORSES SECTIONS C AND D

BROUGHTON

One of the oldest Welsh Cob Studs in the UK, the Broughton Stud was founded by the late J.A. Smith, David's father, and the prefix comes from the name of the hamlet which is their family home. When David's father passed away in 1981 David Smith and Alison Jones took over the Cobs and the Broughton Stud.

Amongst the horses they have at the stud, is *Llanarth Rheinallt [Llanarth Meredith Ap Braint* x *Llanarth Rhalou* x *Llanarth Flying Comet],* purchased in 1982 from the Llanarth Sale. David and Alison showed him in-hand and then, when he was a four year-old, Elfed and Carol Isaac broke him to ride and showed him lightly under saddle. He was second at the Royal Welsh in a large Ridden Stallion class. In 1986 they purchased *Llanarth Welsh Flyer* from Mr and Mrs Len Bigley; he is by *Llanarth Lord Nelson* and out of *Llanarth Sian. Llanarth Welsh Flyer* went to Mr and Mrs Heppenstall in 1996 when he was Ridden Champion at the Royal Welsh and qualified for Olympia at the Yorkshire Show. Both *Llanarth Rheinallt* and *Llanarth Welsh Flyer* have proved themselves under saddle.

David and Alison have also had much success in showing their Cobs in-hand. In 1992 they were International Champion at Peterborough with the black Section D mare, *Broughton Black Lady [Cefncoch Victor* x *Broughton Magic].* They have also enjoyed much success with other people's Cobs as they do take show liveries on a small scale.

Broughton Welsh Cobs ride and compete in Performance classes. *Broughton True Briton [Llanarth True Briton* x *Broughton Port],* a chestnut gelding, was Champion at the Royal of England and the Royal Welsh in the same year. *Broughton Roxanne* was Champion at the Royal of England, 2000 and has competed successfully in Working Hunter Pony Classes, Hunter Trials and Ridden Showing classes. *Broughton Diplomat [Parc Welsh Flyer* x *Llanarth Glyau],* a chestnut stallion, qualified for Wembley and Olympia as a four year-old, achieving Best of Breed at Olympia. He also qualified for Olympia 2000.

The other Cobs that have competed and are still doing so are, *Broughton Eleri,* a full sister to *Roxanne,*

Welsh Cob stallion: *Kallista Russell,* ridden by Caroline Meyer
Photo by Bristow

Section B: *Rhoson Sionc*
Photo by Richard Miller

Section B: *Gayfields Love Potion no. Nine,* Gayfield Stud, USA
Photo by O'neill

Section B stallion: *Baledon Commanchero*
Photo by Anthony Reynolds

Section B: *Sianwood Silvermine,* rider Philippa James
Photo by Anthony Reynolds

Welsh Cob stallion: *Derwen Quartz,* driven by Ifor Lloyd
Photo by M. Lloyd

Welsh Cob Stallion: *Abergavenny jr in Holland.*
rider *Evaline de Gruyter*

International grade showjumper *Mister Woppitt*
(Penlanganol Jasper), rider Geoff Glazzard
Photo by Anthony Reynolds

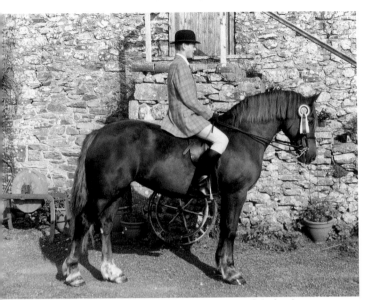

Welsh Cob mare: *Derwen Rosa,* rider Dyfed Lloyd
Photo by M. Lloyd

Welsh Cob: *Bukkenburg Gloss,* Medway Stud. South Africa.
Photo by Bristow

Welsh Cob stallion: *Synod Robert Black,* Joan Thomas Driving.
Photo by Hilary Cotter

Advanced Event Horse: Welsh Cob *Maesmynach Midnight Flyer*
Photo by John Britter

Welsh Cob mares, sisters *Kentchurch Request* (chestnut) and *Kentchurch Rhapsody*. Photo by Anthony Reynolds

Welsh Cob Section D: *Kentchurch Destiny*
Photo by Anthony Reynolds

Welsh Part-Bred: *Ascot China Doll*, Australia
Photo by Gary Jameson

Welsh Mountain Pony: *Ovington Xanadu*
Photo by Hilary Cotter

Welsh Cob stallion: *Derwen Two Rivers* in Denmark, rider Karin Fieldbo

Welsh Cob stallion: *Cascob Flying Colours, Brandon Laufer Driving*
Photo courtesy of Brian Richman, Ontario, Canada

Welsh Mountain Pony mare: *Rowfantina Old Fashioned*, rider Owen Small. Photo by Real Time Imaging

Penlanganol Vixen (Idle Debutante), Welsh Part-Bred.
Photo by Anthony Reynolds

Ddeusant Diamond champion Ridden Welsh Cob 2000.
ridden by John James. Photo by Anthony Reynolds

Welsh Cob mare: *Broughton Roxanne*
Photo by John Britter Photography

Welsh Mountain Pony: *Cwmbachstel Dion*,
rider Samantha Roberts. Photo by Real Time Imaging

Welsh Cob mare: *Bukkenburg Glenda* in South Africa,
owner Sarah Rose

Broughton Last Express and *Broughton Sadie*, both by *Derwen Paddington Express* and *Broughton Rosanne*, x *Llanarth Welsh Flyer*. The Royal Welsh 1999 saw *Broughton Diplomat* first and *Broughton Last Express* second in a large Junior Ridden Stallion Class.

COY

The Coy Stud of Welsh Cobs, is owned by the Bulman Family who have bred and shown Welsh Cobs for around thirteen years. Sixteen horses are kept within the stud, one stallion, four breeding mares, young stock to bring on to show and sell, a gelding and foals.

The stud mainly shows the stallion, *Clougha Reet Lad [Craignant Flyer* x *Pennardd Iona* x *Tireinon Prince]*, a dark bay, nine years old and standing 15hh, bred by Mick Fitzgerald, Raingills Farm. He has been successfully shown from the age of four with a tremendous list of winnings under his belt. He is also broken to ride and going well. His winnings include: WPCS Youngstock class – third out of twenty eight Cobs; Llandysul Show Champion, 1996 – WPCS bronze medal; Cardigan Show, Champion 1998; Lampeter Stallion Show, Mid Wales Champion 1999 and 2000; Lampeter Show, Champion of the Field, 1999 and WPCS bronze medal; Capel Bangor Show, Champion, 1999, also Mountain and Moorland Champion; CWPCS show, Reserve Male Champion 2000. He has also been featured on the front cover of *Horse and Hound* from the Royal of England Show.

The stud shows very successfully under saddle, in particular *Maesyrawel Trotting Will [Nebo More Magic* x *Pennardd Iona* x *Nebo More Magic]*, a fourteen year-old bay gelding, bred by Mr Davies, Tregaron. Shown in In-Hand, Under Saddle, Trekking and Novelty classes since 1989. *Will* is a veteran in the shows. Some of his winnings include: Trekking Classes – Royal Welsh, 1995, 1997 and Champion in 1999; Royal Welsh Reserve Champion 1996 and 1998; WPCS Performance Award Champion 1997, 1998 and 1999; Champion, Lampeter Show 1998 and 1999 and also in previous years. *Maesyrawel Trotting Will* has won so many rosettes throughout the eleven years the Stud have shown him that they are too numerous to mention.

DERWEN

One of the largest and best-known of the Welsh Cob, Section D studs, The Derwen International Stud was started in 1944 by E. Roscoe Lloyd, whose father was one of the founder members of the Welsh Pony and Cob Society in 1903. The foundation mare of the stud was the grand old Section D mare, *Dewi Rosina*, who was sired by *Blaenwaun True Briton*.

The stud is presently owned and run by Mr and Mrs Ifor and Myfanwy Lloyd and their son Dyfed, who has enjoyed many successes in the show ring riding his own Welsh Cob mare, *Derwen Rosa*.

Around a hundred horses are kept at the stud and this number is made up of eight stallions, twenty brood mares, young stock retained for breeding, fifteen geldings (one, two and three year-olds), seventeen foals and the old brood mares. Ifor and Myfanwy also buy in Welsh Cobs to sell on, having broken them to ride and schooled on by the students at the stud. These students come to Derwen from all over Europe.

Usually eight stallions are kept at the stud and at present they are: *Derwen Two Rivers, Derwen Quartz, Derwen Prince Charming, Derwen Duke Of York, Tireinon Step On, Derwen Grand Surprise, Derwen Sea Adventure* and *Derwen Revelation*.

The stud breeds an average of eighteen foals each year, and these foals are of the type that will be useful for work in any sphere. Some of these foals are kept on at the stud and the others are sold for showing and breeding.

The top stallions bred by the stud are *Derwen Replica*, who has won many prizes in-hand and has sired many show winners, and *Derwen Two Rivers*, who was schooled and trained by Karin Fjieldbo from Denmark to Intermediate Dressage standard. *Two Rivers* has won many prizes in showing classes under saddle, also winning jumping and driving events. He has also qualified for the Bronze Buckle long distance riding competition.

One of the top mares bred by the stud, *Derwen Groten Goch*, was three times Prince of Wales Cup winner, which is no easy achievement. The Derwen stud itself has won the Prince of Wales Cup no less than twelve times, which is a superb record, and is

the only stud to have achieved this honour.

The stud engages in as much competition work as is possible, and the current competition horses of the stud are, *Derwen Rosa* by *Derwen Llwynog*, who is by *Nebo Black Magic* and out of *Derwen Rosina*, who is out of *Derwen Rebecca*, who is again by *Nebo Black Magic* and out of *Derwen Rose*. *Derwen Rosa* has won many first prizes under saddle, plus numerous championships, ably ridden by Dyfed Lloyd.

The superb stallion, *Derwen Quartz [Rhystud Flyer* x *Parc Welsh Flyer* out of *Derwen Queen Of Hearts* x *Derwen Llwynog* x *Derwen Queen]*, is another prolific Derwen Stud prizewinner, having achieved many ribbons both in Riding and Driving classes, Dyfed Lloyd making a brilliant job of riding him. *Quartz* was also champion at the 2000 Royal Welsh Show ridden by Maria Leckman.

One of the many mares shown by the stud is *Derwen Danish Girl [Derwen Rosina's Last* x *Derwen Dameg]*. Extremely well-ridden by Beth Proctor, her numerous wins include Supreme Championships and many first prizes.

Derwen horses are not only winners in the UK, but have been consistently in the ribbons abroad. In America, *Derwen True Grit* and *Derwen Denmark* won the pairs driving classes, and *Derwen Tequila* has had numerous wins in Dressage competitions over there. In Sweden, *Derwen Tenessee Express* has been winning in Dressage competitions, and *Derwen Mr. T.* has been a consistent winner in Swedish riding competitions. While in Finland, two of the stud's horses, *Derwen Time Keeper* and *Derwen QC,* have both won many riding competitions. In Germany, *Derwen Reactor* and *Derwen Sherlock Holmes* are making their mark in Driving classes.

Back in the UK, *Derwen Greek Goddess* has brought home many prizes, shown In-Hand by Ifor himself, and he has also successfully shown *Derwen Two Rivers* in numerous Driving competitions.

Two Danish riders spent many years at Derwen, working with Welsh Cobs before returning to Denmark, producing their own stock based on Derwen blood lines. Tove Virkelyst from Sabrow, won the International Show in Sweden in 1998 with *Badentoy Villeam*, a Section C black gelding, born in 1987, and Karin Fjeildbo is winning with a second mare by *Derwen Grand Surprise*, who is out of *Derwen Dancing River*.

Derwen has, over the years, exported many Welsh Cobs to Denmark, Switzerland, France, Canada, Norway, The Netherlands, Japan, Malta, USA, Austria, Russia, Finland, Belgium, Pakistan, Sweden, Australia, Germany and Italy, and all are successfully competing in their own spheres. Recently Derwen has exported two horses to Spain: *Derwen Cantona*, a Welsh Mountain stallion recently sold to Pascal Gonzalez of Valencia, and *Derwen Grand Finale*, a Section D colt, sold to Paul and Sue Horey, of the Ribble Valley Stud, in Alicante.

Derwen International Welsh Cob Centre offers students from all countries the opportunity to spend time at the Centre working with the Welsh Cobs, with a chance to compete on the top horses there.

GRANGE
JOAN THOMAS

The Grange Stud was started by Mr Dill Thomas who kept the Welsh Cob stallion, *Llwynog-y-Garth*, bought from Roscoe Lloyd, Derwen Stud, and also a yard of his stallions. He also dealt in all kinds of horses at home and abroad.

Joan began her career with horses at the age of four with Leading Rein showing on a pony called *Revel Spring Song*, plus whatever pony that happened to come along. At the age of twelve Joan drove *Llwynog-y-Garth* in a show wagon winning the Applause Cup at the Royal Welsh Show. She also had a Ridden Show Pony which she rode at the Horse of the Year Show in a 13.2hh pony class and was placed eighth. Joan tried show jumping but she did not enjoy it very much so gave that up. She started private driving with *Llwynog-y-Grange* who was bred on the farm and is still alive today aged thirty four years. Among other breeds Joan had for driving was the Welsh Cob Stallion, *Rhosmeirch Fly Away*, which she sold to Swains of Stretton and they sponsored her for three years. She has also been sponsored by Pretty Polly tights and Memory Lane Cakes, and in recent times, Brightwells.

Joan enters mostly Private Driving classes and Welsh Cob classes in a show wagon. During 2000 Joan showed the Welsh Cob stallions, *Synod Robert*

Black, Tireinon Conquest and *Broodfield Black Prince,* in Private Drive classes and *Derwen Sea Adventure* (owned by Mrs Myfanwy Lloyd, Derwen Stud) in a show wagon.

Synod Robert Black enjoyed an impressive season during 2000, winning 1st and Champion at Newark and Notts. At Smiths Lawn he qualified for HOYS, coming sixth with five Hackneys in front of him. At the Royal Welsh he was 1st and Champion and 1st at Essex County and also Kent County. He was again 1st and Champion at Peterborough, 2nd and Reserve Champion at Royal Windsor and the same again at Leicester City, amongst many other wins at smaller shows over the summer.

KENTCHURCH

Kentchurch Stud in Hampshire, is one of the biggest studs of Welsh Cobs in the UK producing performance Cobs. It is owned and run by Mrs Anne Vestey who has been involved with horses and ponies all her life. As children, Anne and her two sisters lived on a farm and were lucky enough to have ponies to ride, later having lessons from an ex-military Instructor at boarding school, and during the holidays had lessons with Miss Sybil Smith at the famous Cadogan Riding School.

In 1953 Anne purchased a Welsh Mountain pony from a Miss McAlpine, and when the pony was outgrown she was covered by *Coed Coch Socyn.* In 1958 *Kentchurch Silver Slipper* was born and so was the Kentchurch prefix. *Slipper* produced many

foals, some more memorable than others, but when in 1970 Anne married an international racing driver who was not exactly 'horse' minded – unless it was horsepower – her father sent *Slipper* to Anne as her 'dowry'.

It was by chance that Anne met, and became friends with, Dan and Diana Haak who at that time bred Section As, Bs and Ds. *Slipper* had gone to their Uplands Stud to visit *Clan Pip*, and later *Coed Coch Pela*, when Anne began to find the Cobs looking tempting, and fancied one to hack around the farm.

Unfortunately Uplands Stud did not have a ridden Cob for sale but Anne fell for a gentle, khaki-coloured brood mare and, unable to resist her, purchased her and arranged to have her covered by *Parc Commando. Llanarth Rhuddel* was by *Llanarth Meteor* out of *Llanarth Rachel*, and although she was the wrong colour and unbroken, Anne spent many happy summer evenings hacking round the farm.

The following year *Rhuddel* produced *Commandant* who went on to win over a hundred Championships In-Hand and Under Saddle including the Overall Championship for the Welsh Pony and Cob Awards. He also qualified for the Taylor Woodrow Dressage Finals at Goodwood and led the Welsh Cob display at Olympia in 1983. He stood at stud for many years with Mabel Stuart-Hunt at the Exton Stud and was ridden by Kate Harris (*née* Chapell), when she was fourteen years old. *Commandant* sired *Kentchurch Dynasty* who Kate owned and which qualified for Olympia twice and won the Royal of England Ridden Welsh Cob class. *Kentchurch Dallas* won the South of England, Royal Cornwall, third at the Royal Welsh In-Hand, and also won driving and riding classes in Denmark and is still breeding at Kentchurch. *Kentchurch Destiny*, another full sister, who won Champion Ridden Welsh Cob twice at the Royal of England as well as Champion at the Royal Welsh, is also at Kentchurch.

Commandant later stood at Catherston Stud after the death of Mabel Stuart-Hunt and continued to produce many winners both pure-bred and part-bred. His part-bred son *Exton Sea Lord* regularly qualified for Wembley and Olympia Show Jumping and another part-bred *Kentchurch Punch* won the WPCS Award for Dressage. Anne has given *Commandant* to a friend in Denmark where he is spending his twilight years running out with mares and foals. His first Danish-bred foal recently won her first show, first time out.

Commandant's two full sisters, *Catrin* and *Cerys*, both qualified for Olympia four times and won Best of Breed. *Catrin* also won the Royal of England Under Saddle and the South of England In-Hand. Anne sold her in foal and she produced *Taiforgan Bonheddwr* who has won the new prestigious Ridden Mountain and Moorland Championship at Wembley. *Cerys* is favourite at Kentchurch and has, after three colt foals, produced a filly, a clone of

herself named *Celebration*. *Cloud*, who won Olympia, is a half brother to *Cerys* and full brother to *Chelsea*, also an Olympia qualifier. *Charm*, *Charisma* and *Chaos* are all prolific winners, and *Kentchurch Chime*, who stands in America, is a leading Dressage horse and Driving Cob (see pages 110-1) is full brother to *Commandant*. In all *Rhuddel* had fourteen foals, seven colts and seven fillies, all prizewinners.

Rhuddel was later joined by *Rhiangel,* her full sister, who produced many stunning foals including *Rhapsody, Request* and *Whisper*, full sisters by *Llanarth Welsh Warrior*, all of whom qualified for Olympia. *Request* was Ridden Champion at Olympia having stood Reserve to *Whisper* when she was Champion Ridden at the Royal Welsh. *Llanarth Rhun* who stands at the Scole Stud in Scotland and is a prolific winner Under Saddle and in Harness, as well as In-Hand, is also out of *Llanarth Rhiangel*.

Llanarth Rhalou also came to join her sisters but as a half sister she is by *Llanarth Flying Comet*. Again her children have excelled. She is the dam of *Llanarth Rheinallt* who won the Royal Welsh Ridden class and stands at the Broughton Stud, and of *Llanarth Rhagori* who won a tremendous amount In-Hand and Under Saddle including the East of England and Royal Highland In-Hand and the Championship Under Saddle at the Royal Welsh. *Kentchurch Cassanova* has returned to Kentchurch having won FEI Internationally driven singles and pairs. He was also Supreme Ridden Champion, ridden by Kate Harris.

The *Llanarth* sisters were joined by *Miranda*, dam of *Mirage* and *Motivation*, as well as *Masquerade*, Anne's Advanced Dressage large Part-Bred who has represented England in Barcelona.

Kentchurch Glory, another daughter of *Commandant*, qualified for Wembley having won the South of England show. She was out of *Scole Welsh Maid*, a daughter of *Llanarth Welsh Warrior*, who twice qualified for Olympia and produced so many wonderful children.

Finally, Anne bought *Llanarth Rhion*, himself a Champion Under Saddle and sire of one of the Wembley finalists, also sire of *Celebration*, to continue these wonderful rare bloodlines created by the late Miss Pauline Taylor. Anne felt it was in the stars to buy *Rhion* as she had bought his dam, *Llanarth Flying Rocket*, a full sister to *Llanarth Flying Comet*, at the last Llanarth sale after the death of Miss Taylor.

Slipper lives on. Having put her daughter, *Kentchurch Silver Pippa*, by *Clan Pip* to *Commandant*, she produced Anne's first Section C, *Kentchurch Silver Cobweb*, a true performance pony who won the Working Hunter class at Northleach. She produced *Silver Cracker* by *Warrior* who she hopes to bring out later under saddle.

MAESMYNACH

Maesmynach Stud is one of the biggest Welsh Cob Studs in the UK, possessing the old blood lines that the Cob was renowned for: the hardiness, the elegance, the intelligence, excellent temperament and performance. The stud is owned by Mr Eric Davies, his wife, and his daughter, Nicola. Eric is a Welsh Pony and Cob Society Council Member as well as the Vice Chairman of the National Stallion Association.

Maesmynach has developed and expanded, and by now approximately a hundred Pure-Bred Welsh Cobs can be seen at the stud. They all possess a character and presence that the true old Cardiganshire Welsh Cob possessed, and within five generations their breeding spans from the beginning of the Stud Book of the WPCS in 1902. Take, for example *Maesmynach Eleri*, dam of *Maesmynach Viking Warrior*. Her sire, *Madeni Welsh Comet*, was foaled in 1955; his sire, *Garabaldi Welsh Flyer*, was foaled in 1939; his sire, *Ceitho Welsh Flyer*, was foaled in 1917; his sire, *Garabaldi Comet 11*, was foaled in 1900 and his sire, *Garabaldi Flyer*, was foaled in 1886.

Therefore the old lines that stood 15.2hh, 15.3hh and 16hh and over are very much seen in the five Home-Bred Maesmynach stallions that stand at stud: *Maesmynach Llwynog*, 15.2hh, *Measmynach King Flyer,* 15hh, *Maesmynach Welsh Flyer,* 16hh, *Measmynach Cymro Coch*, 15.3hh, and *Maesmynach Viking Warrior*, 15.3hh. All these stallions ride and all hunt by side.

Maesmynach stock have been sold to compete and perform in many spheres. They are part of Driving teams in Britain, and abroad, competing at National and International level; for example, *Lliedi Rhyfelwr*, by *Maesmynach Viking Warrior*, who has won Championships and Reserve Championships at the National Driving Championships at Necarne, Northern Ireland Driving Trials, at Loughry.

'To be born Welsh is to be born priviledged'. An old saying with an eternal message. Indeed, the British Horse Foundation in their dinner at the British Equine Event confirmed the benefit of Welsh Breeds or, more specifically, of the old Welsh Bloodlines, when *Maesmynach Viking Warrior* won their Award for the Top Stallion Born in or after 1985 by progeny winnings (show jumping).

Maesmynach Viking Warrior is the first Native Breed to have ever won such an award, fending off competition from the Thoroughbreds, the Warmbloods, Hanoverians and all other foreign and Native Breeds. The stallion is no stranger to the Royal Welsh Show, having been the lead highway robber with three other Maesmynach stallions in the Pageant held by Ceredigion during their feature year.

A Gala Celebrity Evening was held in conjunction with the Awards at the Royal of England Show Ground at Stoneleigh where all prize-winning stock were displayed including *Maesmynach Viking Warrior* and his progeny group.

The progeny group included *Penlanganol Jasper (Mr. Whoppit)*, a Grade A Show Jumper ridden by Geoff Glazzard, a runner up in the Thomas Bates six and seven year-old final at Wembley, and winner of the award for the Best British Bred Horse in the competition. Also present was *Midnight Flyer*, a half brother to *Maesmynach Viking Warrior*, an advanced eventer who is regularly competing with Tiny Clapham, an Olympic rider, and *Penlanganol Vixen (Idle Debutante)*, a Grade C Show Jumper, whose dam is also the dam of *Mr. Whoppitt*.

The recognition of *Maesmynach Viking Warrior* and the celebration of a Welsh Breed, confirms the stamina, presence and intelligence of the old bloodlines, as noted in *Horse and Hound*; '*Maesmynach Viking Warrior* broke new ground when he claimed the British Horse Foundation Award'.

MENAI

Menai Stud, now owned and run by Peter and Anne Jones, was founded by Peter's grandfather, the late Williams Jones, at the turn of the century, with registrations in the first few volumes of the WPCS Stud Books.

The famous Welsh Mountain Pony Stallion, *Bleddfa Shooting Star*, covered *Clettwr Polly* in 1913; the resulting progeny, *Menai Queen Bess,* was born in 1914. *Queen Bess* was covered with the small Cob stallion *Welsh Rebound*, producing *Menai Queen Bee* in 1937. This outstanding mare was a prolific show winner, and it was on *Queen Bee* that Peter learnt to ride. Covered with *Caradog Clwyd* she produced first of all the bay stallion *Menai Ceredig*, who was purchased by the Llanarth Stud where he sired among others such stallions as *Llanarth Rhys* and the spectacular *Llanarth Meteor*. Her second mating with *Caradog Llwyd* produced the dun mare, *Menai Ceridwen*, who produced many good ponies for Menai, including *Menai Carys* by the seven times Royal Welsh Champion *Teify Brightlight*. *Ceridwen*'s son, *Menai Fury*, was one of the first ponies, and probably the best, that Peter has had the privilege of showing. One of the great goers of all time, *Fury* was a real crowd pleaser despite being second at the Royal Welsh no fewer than five times, before eventually winning the stallion class. He is probably the most famous and certainly the most influential Section C stallion of all time, siring more Royal Welsh winners than any other stallion, and whose stamp he has left on the Section Cs for generations. His two sons, the brothers, *Menai Bonheddwr*, who runs out with his mares at Menai, and the inimitable *Menai Furious*, are carrying on the lineage at the stud. *Furious* excelled under saddle, winning numerous prizes, ridden and produced by Katy Girdler (see page 78). *Menai Bonheddwr* began his career under saddle in 1999 in the hands of Jo Bond and the stud has great expectations for him in the future, now with Katy Girdler at Ffrethi. His daughter, *Menai Lady Conspicuous*, crowned a successful showing career both in Youngstock

classes and as a young mare when she was judged Female Champion and Reserve Overall Supreme Champion at the 1999 Royal Welsh.

It was a tragic loss to the stud and also the breed, to lose the twice Lampeter Stallion Show Welsh Cob Champion *Menai Sparkling Comet* at such an early age. *Comet* was out of *Menai Lady Corona*, a daughter of *Trefaes Spark*, who left his mark at Menai, and by *Tyhen Comet*, who was Supreme Champion at the 1989 Royal Welsh, judged by Peter's father. William Jones was the last person to judge both the Cobs and the Ponies of Cob Type at the Royal Welsh on the same day. There are four of *Sparkling Comet*'s daughters at the Stud, and two of his half sisters out of the same mare. *Menai Sparkling Duchess* and *Menai Sparkling Lady*, both by the Prince of Wales Cup winner *Nebo Daniel*. *Sparkling Lady* is unique having won her class at the Royal Welsh as a yearling, two and three year-old. Her first foal, *Menai Sparkling Magic*, won his class at the Royal Welsh before being exported to Germany, where not only has he been National Champion on several occasions, but was also Champion Welsh Cob at the International Show in Denmark in 1992, and in Sweden in 1998. *Menai Flying Lady* is *Sparkling Lady*'s first daughter, by *Thorneyside Flyer*. This young mare is now in the capable hands of Trish Hardy of Ontario, where she is excelling in Dressage against all breeds. At present there are twenty Welsh Cob brood mares at Menai and at present the senior stallion is *Menai Sparkling*

Image, the eight year-old son of *Menai Sparkling Comet*. Rarely shown due to stud commitments, he is much in demand on account of his exceptional stock.

Much of the credit for putting the stud onto such a sound footing must go to Peter's father who was responsible for re-introducing the Section As to the stud with a few select mares some thirty years ago. *Gredington Asa,* son of *Coed Coch Planed,* won Championships at all the major shows. Another stallion that left his mark was *Twyford Santa,* son of *Twyford Gurkha,* who was sold on to Australia. *Twyford Marchog* left some superb brood mares before also going to Australia. The stud was very fortunate in being able to bring *Friars Ranger* back from Denmark for the latter part of his life, and he sired some outstanding brood mares. Now there are thirty Section A brood mares and six stallions at the stud.

Sadly no longer with the stud, *Revel Japhet* retired from the show ring as Supreme Champion of all Breeds at the Royal Welsh. His influence continues through his outstanding daughters, and it will not go unrecognised. Neither will the contributions of *Menai Smartie, Friars Sion, Friars Sianco, Bengad Whitebeam,* and the young stallion, *Friars Generous,* whose colt foal broke the record for being the highest-priced colt sold at public auction at the stud's 1996 reduction sale.

Menai Stud will endeavour to continue breeding ponies and Cobs in all Sections that are of true Welsh Type and character, and with the conformation and straight movement to excel in any sphere.

NEBO

Nebo Stud, as it is known today, was formed when Geraint and Mary Jones got married in 1961 but the Nebo prefix was used for registered Welsh Ponies and Cobs as far back as 1918. The foundation mare was a wedding present, the brood mare *Tyngwndwn Mathrafal Lady*, and Tyngwndwn was Geraint's prefix prior to his marriage. This prefix is used today by their daughter Lisa and her husband, while Owen, their son, shares the prefix Nebo. This valuable brood mare became an asset to the stud. She was the dam of *Nebo Black Magic*, a stallion known worldwide, and very seldom does his line of breeding not appear in the extended pedigrees of most of today's Cobs. Amongst others this mare also produced *Nebo Princess Ann*, the dam of many champions including *Nebo Daniel*.

Amongst the present Stud stallions are the Section C *Nebo Bouncer*, by *Nebo Brenin*. Born in 1981, he had the looks of making a top-class stallion from the first days of his life. Unfortunately he lost his mother at the age of six weeks but this did not hold him back for, as a yearling, he went to his first show and finished Reserve Champion. He travelled to a number of shows with great success, his wins that year included such shows as the Royal Welsh, Lampeter Stallion Show, Glanusk and the NPS, to name just a few. Over the years *Bouncer* has given the stud enormous pleasure both in the show ring and by siring top quality ponies. He has been Champion at Lampeter Stallion Show five times and won the Royal Welsh on seven occasions, bringing the Chetwynd Perpetual Trophy to Nebo four times. In 1988 he won Supreme Champion at the Royal Welsh and represented the show at the Horse of the Year Show at Wembley. He has been in the sire rating charts since the age of four and won for the first time in 1992, an achievement he has repeated five times since. Some of his noted progeny are, *Hengwys Tywysog*, *Tyngwndwn Daylight*, *Tyngwndwn Mischief* and *Hafodyrynys Cariad*.

Nebo Daniel, foaled in 1976, was the first foal out of *Nebo Princess Ann*. His future success could be visualised from his early days as he would spend endless hours trotting around the paddock in great style, well away from his dam. He began his showing career as a foal but came into the limelight as a yearling. He was shown with great success both in England and Wales until he was retired in 1990 after winning the Supreme Champion at Lampeter Stallion Show. He left his career in the show ring at the age of fourteen years after being Champion at most of the County shows. In 1988 he won the George Prince of Wales Trophy for the Champion Welsh Cob at the Royal Welsh. He was Male Champion in 1986 and 1989. In 1987 he was Supreme Champion at the Three Counties Show, Malvern. He represented the show at the Horse of

the Year Show in the Lloyds In-Hand Champion. He also won the WPCS sire ratings on several occasions. Along with his showing success *Daniel* is also a terrific stockgetter, producing mares and stallions of the greatest calibre. Some of his notable progeny include *Nebo Prince*, *Nebo Victoria*, *Northleach Danielle*, *Tewgoed Mari* and also *Tewgoed Janet* and *Tynybryn Miss Poppedyn*, Supreme Champion at the 1999 Danish Grading Show. Along with his sire, *Nebo Brenin*, *Daniel* is also a great producer of Section Cs. Among his progeny are *Nebo Rachel* and *Neuaddparc Welsh Maid*.

SIANWOOD

John and Anne James of the Sianwood Stud (see pages 81-2) were continually being asked to break and school horses and ponies which were sent to them. One evening in August 1997 John and Ann received a telephone call from a Mr Thomas who had three Welsh Cobs he wanted broken for the Cob sale in October. They duly arrived by lorry, somewhat bewildered having never been away from home, all looking extremely well but naturally unfit. In fact they were particularly nice Cobs, one especially was *Ddeusant Diamond*.

As John became more familiar with Mr and Mrs Thomas and as *Diamond* responded to her education, it was unanimously agreed to withdraw her from the sale and to introduce her to a career under saddle in the show ring. Neville and Daphne Thomas had moved to Llanddeusant from Sussex in

1987. In Sussex they had bred Welsh Cobs successfully under the Loxwood prefix and had bred *Loxwood Dusky Maid*, x *Verwig Matharafal, Diamond*'s dam. February 1998 was *Diamond*'s first show, a very large Novice Class near Haverfordwest. She won comfortably and this was followed by a Championship at the Forest of Dean together with several other wins and Championships. At the Royal Welsh she was called into first place and finished third. Her first season terminated with a great deal of silver and red ribbons for her very proud owners. Her second season followed suit, repeating her Royal Welsh practice of being called in first but this time she finished second. Her third season in 2000 saw the procedure being repeated again but not only did she remain first but she became Female Champion and finally Overall Ridden Champion. Not content with this she rewarded her owner's efforts by becoming Champion Ridden Mountain and Moorland at Monmouth County Show, thereby qualifying for the Horse of the Year Show at Wembley where she finished sixth.

Sianwood Stud has bred, bought and produced many lovely ponies over the years, not forgetting Philippa and David's Lead Rein/First Ridden winner, *Bengad Banksia [Bengad Nepeta x Bengad Buttercup]*, the Reserve Supreme Champion Royal Welsh winning yearling, *Sianwood Star Turn [Cusop Disciplin x Sianwood Jazmyn]*, *Sianwood Sylvester*,

Royal Welsh Part-Bred winner, and many more. At Sianwood it is a family and a team effort.

SYNOD

Cerdin and Doreen Jones, and their daughter Amanda, own and run Synod which they adopted as a prefix in 1969 after their marriage. Cerdin had been breeding Section Cs in partnership with his father, D.I. Jones of the Tydi Stud, and in 1967, *Tydi Rosina* produced *Tydi Rosemary*, x *Hendy Brenin*. In 1969 *Rosina* gave birth to *Rosemary*'s half brother, the incomparable *Synod William x Menai Fury*. *William* was a great sire, winning the progeny class at the Royal Welsh ten times, and a successful show pony, winning the Overall Championship at the Royal Welsh, four times. He left the Stud an outstanding line of four stallions, *Roger, Reagan, Ranger* and *Rum Punch*, all out of *William*'s half sister, *Tydi Rosemary*. This close mating was largely due to the scarcity of Section C stallions at the time, but was a great success.

Synod Roger is a real character and a prolific show winner. In 1997 he won the Championship at the Royal of England and in the next class, Mrs Deirdre Colville won the Driving with *Synod Cerdin* x *Menai Fury*. *Cerdin* won a brilliant treble that year by winning the Royal Highland and the Royal Welsh, while he was also Supreme in Driving Trials, winning at Holker Hall, Lowther and the Scottish. He joined *Synod Rob Roy, Synod Glenda* and *Synod Princess Charming* in a spectacular team of four chestnuts with white socks, driven by Wyn Colville.

1984 saw *Synod Roger* qualify for the Lloyds In-Hand at Wembley, as did the stud's Section A, *Brierwood Rocket*.

Synod Roger won the 1998 Welsh International Show in Brussels, as well as the Royal Welsh, and *Synod Ranger*, who had been bought by Mrs Colville, was Champion at Lampeter Stallion Show as a yearling. *Synod Rum Punch* was not shown until 1998 as being such a good stock getter he was left with his mares; however, he carried all before him in his first season, being Champion, shown by Len Bigley, at the Royal Welsh in 1999.

Synod does not show mares very often as they dislike taking foals to shows too much, however the stud is certainly well-known all over the world for the showing results of its stallions, both the ones retained at the stud and the ones that have been sold on to new homes in the UK and abroad.

TEIFI

In 1914 *Teifi Comet*, a chestnut stallion, was registered in the WPCS Stud Book by T. Jones and the breeder was D. S. Davies. After years of being used by various members, the Teifi prefix was registered in 1962 to Mr D.E. Williams of Lampeter, a friend of the family. Teifi was then transferred to Stuart Lloyd in 1989.

In the Autumn of 1981 Stuart attended the Royal Welsh Cob Sale, where a bay colt foal caught his eye; he bought him; his name was *Dimbeth Sion*. Out of *Parc Primrose*, a typey mare by *Parc Welsh Flyer*, the sire was *Parc Dafydd*. *Sion*'s bloodlines are dominated by *Parc Lady* and *Pentre Eiddwen Comet*, two of the most influential cobs of modern times.

Sion was a natural from the beginning. On his show debut as a yearling he was placed second at Glanusk Stallion Show, the start of a successful two years where he was only shown in-hand. In the Autumn of his second year he was mouthed and long-reined and in the November he was backed. In December he was pulling a chain harrow and on Christmas Day *Sion* was being driven around the streets of Lampeter. The following day he was ridden to hounds. Over the next few years *Sion* was shown In-Hand and became a Premium Stallion on several occasions. It was then that Stuart and his partner, 'D', decided to spend the winter preparing him for performance classes.

Sion subsequently qualified for Peterborough at his first attempt, won many Championships and also had wins in Dressage and Show Jumping. History was made in the Welsh Cob classes at the 1997 Royal Welsh when *Sion* won the Driving class on the Wednesday, and on the Thursday morning, with over forty entries, he won the Ridden class. This was a unique achievement as no horse had ever won this 'Ride and Drive' double in ninety five years of our National Show. In fact the closest that any Cob had come to achieving this was in 1994 when *Sion* won the Driving class and was fourth Under Saddle. To honour such a feat, the Welsh Pony and Cob Society presented *Sion* with the Daisy Broderick Memorial Trophy, an honorary award for his contribution towards promoting the Welsh Breeds.

TYSSUL

Established in 1953 by Tommi and Bessie Lewis, the Tyssul Stud evolved from the acquisition of a Cob mare, *Tyssul Poppy*. Over the next ten years ponies were bought and sold, but it was the purchase of the Section B stallion *Treharne Peregrine* that enticed Tommi and his younger son, Alun, to enter the show ring. Winning the Stallion Class at Lampeter Stallion Show with *Tim*, as he was affectionately called, meant that the showing bug had bitten and there was no turning back.

Versatility was always a necessity with the ponies, from the Cob mare who carried the milk churns, to the brood mares that the children hunted. In the middle sixties, Tommi set his sights at producing top quality Section C ponies with a temperament that was conducive with adaptability. *Meiarth Llinos* was the dam of so many versatile sons. *Tussul Cerdin* was born in 1969. He took the Youngstock Premium at Lampeter as a two year-

old, after which his talents were targeted at performance events. He rewarded his owner by winning the Section C Stallion Performance Awards in 1974/5, being reserve overall Ride and Drive Champion in 1974, and Champion in 1975. *Tyssul Cardi* won the Royal Welsh in 1970 as a foal and again as a two year-old. He then became the first Section C to be exported to Australia.

Tyssul Coram is well-known as a Supreme In-Hand stallion, winning both Section C and Palomino Championships, but he also won Under Saddle and Driving classes. He competed in both Show Wagon and Private Driving classes. His progeny have proved to be the most versatile of Section C ponies. *Coram* covered Tommi's cousin Jimmy's mare, *Orllwyn Moli*, and in 1979 *Moli* produced a Palomino colt, *Jona*, who, under the guidance of George and Mary Davies, won many Ride and Drive classes, but shone in the Private Driving. He is the only pony of any breed to complete the ultimate double of winning both the Supreme Show Champion at Smith's Lawn and the Thimbleby and Shoreland National Private Driving Championships in 1992. In 1985 *Orllwyn Coram* came into the world. He started winning as a yearling In-Hand and continued in his father's footsteps. In his prime *Coram* totalled thirteen Championships in the 1989 season, winning the Premium Class at Lampeter for three successive years. *Coram* has been placed at the Royal Welsh in all three disciplines, and transported brides to weddings.

Tyssul ponies have the gift of longevity. *Jona* is still competing at twenty one years of age and *Tyssul Mai* is still winning the Veteran Driving class for Ann Reynolds at the grand old age of twenty nine years. Tommi believed that a true Section C was most definitely a pony, a pony of Cob Type and not a small Cob. This belief is continued by Alun. The quality, conformation and temperament have not changed in any way over the decades. Tommi was liked and trusted by everyone in the Society, his judging invitations culminating at the Royal Welsh Show in 1988. Four months later Tommi died from a massive stroke. Although sadly missed his spirit lives on in the Tyssul ponies.

CHAPTER TWELVE

PERFORMANCE HORSES AND PONIES ACROSS THE WORLD

ASCOT STUD
AUSTRALIA
QUALITY RIDING PONIES. WELSH
SECTION B. WELSH PART-BREDS

Ascot Stud and Show Stables are run by Kerry Muller and Melanie McGuire-Muller, located in Victoria, the home of the senior stallion, *Gaylord of Ascot* and future sire, *Ascot Classic Silk*. The Ascot Stud has been established for twenty years and runs a small group of select mares headed by the foundation mare, *Downland Solitaire*. The main emphasis at the stud is to breed ponies in small numbers of the highest quality and producing a distinct 'look and type' of pony, suitable to carry a saddle. Breeding stock ranges from 12.1hh to 14.2hh. The stud has professionally and consistently produced, bred and exhibited its own Riding Ponies at Royal Show, State and National Level for many wins and Championships in-hand and under saddle over the years.

The pinnacle for Ascot Stud was the arrival of the Welsh Section B mare *Downland Solitaire*, bred in the purple *Downland Chevalier* x *Downland Camelia* x *Downland Dauphin*. *Solitaire* was lightly shown, winning Supreme Champion Welsh B at the Victoria Stud Show, and a year later judged Supreme Welsh Exhibit of all sections at the same show with *Ascot Design*, x *Baughurst William of Orange*, at foot. She has produced six foals for Ascot Stud and every one has either won or been a Championship winner at a Royal. *Solitaire* has also produced four Champion Riding Pony Youngstock Females at the Victorian Riding Pony Pageant, the state-show run for Riding Ponies. These are:

Ascot Satin Doll, x *Percy of Paxhall*, who was Supreme Youngstock Exhibit In-Hand, also National Two Year-Old of the Year, Melbourne Royal Royal Champion riding Pony Filly at three, also Champion Welsh Section B Filly at Melbourne Royal as a yearling. She also amassed many Saddle wins, including being a Barastoc Saddle Pony of the Year finalist twice, before being retired to stud at five years.

Ascot China Doll, x *Owendale Percival*, who was Supreme Champion Youngstock In-Hand and Grand Champion In-Hand. She also won her Three Year-

Old Filly class at Melbourne Royal and achieved many wins Under Saddle, including Melbourne Royal, Victorian Royal Welsh and a Barastoc Large Saddle Pony finalist.

Ascot Lisa Marie, x *Strinesdale Matador*, has been Champion Filly, Supreme Youngstock In-Hand as yearling and Champion Filly as a two year-old amongst other wins. She has also gained many agricultural championships under saddle and is now leased to a twelve year-old girl to continue her ridden career.

Ascot Satin Doll is the first *Solitaire* grand-daughter to carry on a second generation. Her first foal, *Ascot Classic Silk*, x *Westacre Concerto*, will be retained as a future sire. The stud is fortunate to have a number of foals bred via AI in the wings to carry the breeding programme into the future.

It is felt that the stud is almost self sufficient for the future, with a wealth of the world's best blood already brought into the fold and with the use of frozen semen from some of the best pony stallions over a strong mare base. The stud feels that it now has a strong genetic pool to breed the type of pony they like and to fulfil their vision.

The aim at Ascot Stud has always been to produce a very distinctive look about the ponies they breed and show. The main purpose of the breeding programme is to produce ponies that will excel both In-Hand and Under Saddle. Temperament in the ponies is also important which is why the Welsh Section B blood is maintained throughout.

GAYFIELDS WELSH PONIES
USA

Gayfields Welsh Pony Stud started with the first crop of foals in Arkansas in 1969 and, as Gail and Arthur Thomson expected to be Section A breeders, to that end they purchased *Coed Coch Prydydd [Coed Coch Glyndwr x Coed Coch Pioden]* as a herd stallion. The first mare were *Downland Icicle [Downland Epic x Downland Iolanthe]*. Then came *Criban Old Silver [Bowdler Brewer x Criban Old Gold]*; next was *Pickwick Shan [Rockburn Toy Soldier x Shan Cwilt]*, and *Honor Pennant [Merrie Mill's Pennant x Hendre Dyddgu, Snowdon Tywysog x Snowdon Sylvia 11]*. Gail's favourites bred from this herd all matured to 12.3hh and inadvertently become Section B breeders; so, as there were few Bs in their area they switched emphasis, keeping *Criban Old Silver* and her daughters and some daughters of *Honor Pennant* and *Pickwick Shan*.

Although other stallions were used at the Stud in 1981, *Sleight of Hand [Milncroft Spun Gold x Coed Coch Olwen]*, was imported and also *Pendock Masterpiece [Solway Master Bronze x Pendock Pruedence]*. Retaining some daughters of *Masterpiece* the stud is currently using *Sleight of Hand* and one of his grandsons.

Over the years Gayfields Welsh Ponies have won many High Score Championships, Supreme Championships of shows, etc, but the most important of accolades won are the Legion of Merit Awards. The Welsh Pony and Cob Society of

America keeps points on sanctioned shows for Individual Legion of Merit, Sire Legion of Merit and Dam Legion of Merit. So far a total of thirty have been awarded, twelve individual, nine Sire and nine Dam, with *Sleight of Hand*'s award being the first won. Three of *Sleight*'s daughters and a grand-daughter have individuals LOMs and six of the nine honoured mares have won theirs through *Sleight of Hand*'s sons and daughters, including five of Gayfields' own mares and one they bred but sold. *Pendock Masterpiece* also has a Sire Legion of Merit, won for him by offspring sired while he was at Gayfields. A sire LOM requires that a stallion amasses a total of 2,500 points with at least five individual offspring having a minimum of 300 points each. So far *Sleight*'s offspring have won 33,000 with over 30 individuals having 300 points each. His close competitor has under 7,000 points and six qualifying offspring. *Sleight* has now received the first Award of Excellence and the highest award the Society bestows, the Order of the Dragon. *Sleight* is also the only pony or Cob to be Supreme Champion at an American National Welsh Show more than once and has done so three times. (see pages 83-4)

Gail and Arthur agree that using Section A foundation stock for their Section B herd has allowed them to keep Welsh Type and bone while allowing them to attain an average of 13hh to 13.2hh ponies that can perform well for older children and adults alike. They have around fifty ponies at present and expect ten to fifteen foals each year. Gayfields' Welsh ponies continue to win Riding, Driving and Hunter Championships for their current owners.

GLENHAVEN WELSH PONIES AND COBS USA

Glenhaven is owned and run by Suzanne and John Moody and located in Virginia; however, the Glenhaven Stud was started in 1988 by Suzanne. At first it was no easy task to import a 'new' breed into America but now Glenhaven is the largest importer and breeder in the USA, and is nationally renowned due to the extensive advertising, television exposure and the incredible accomplishments of the animals themselves. Also Glenhaven is the only stud in the USA that represents all four Sections of the Stud Book.

Credit must go largely to *Derwen Denmark*, purchased from Robert Manchip in 1992. *Denmark* almost single handedly put, not only Glenhaven, but also Welsh Cobs on the map in the United States. Suzanne distinctly remembers arriving at Open shows, early on in his career, being surrounded by expensive Fresians, Morgans and Standard Breds with her one Cob stallion. They were not at that time viewed as a threat; however, with each progressive Championship to his credit, *Denmark* demanded and received his rightful respect and admiration from their fellow competitors. Since then he has become the yardstick by which both

Open and Welsh competitors measure their own performance. He was one of three Glenhaven Welsh National Champions for 1996 attending only five shows to accomplish this. Taking National Honours with him was *Derwen Tequila*, and *Derwen True Grit*. He is undisputed Driving Champion on the West Coast.

The ponies have also challenged the driving and riding world. *Ceulan Samswn*, a truly outstanding stallion, has a list of firsts that require an abridged version. He and *Ceulan (J) Bubble* represent the Welsh Ponies at their best and stand as ambassadors to prospective buyers.

The popularity of the Cobs exploded and most of the Glenhaven foals are sold before they are born. To fulfil the market demand Suzanne, together with Rose Hardwicke, established the Glenhaven-Tuscany Export Agency and have imported many animals from Derwen, Tuscany, Powysvalley, Hengwm, London, Ceulan, Vimpenny, Forlan, Llanfillo, Archway, Kilvey and Downland. It was because of the increasing demand for Working Hunter and Show Ponies that Sections Bs were imported, amongst them, the legendary Section B stallion *Downland Rembrandt*.

Since Suzanne's marriage to John, who is an equine vet, the stud has relocated to a 220 acre farm in Virginia, which they run with a girl from Scotland. There are now eleven stallions standing at stud. In 1999 the Section A stallion, *Forlan Tarragon*, was high point USA Champion. *Derwen Tequila* was Reserve Champion C/D mare. Glenhaven young stock has also done very well. During 1999 a two year-old Section A filly by *Vimpenny Sweet Sultan* was Supreme Champion at the American Nationals.

Glenhaven has recently imported three more Cobs, *Derwen Danish Girl*, a full sister to Denmark [*Tuscani Arabella*, x *Derwen Railway Express*], as well as a foal Suzanne bred herself in the UK, *Glenhaven American Express* by *Derwen Railway Express*. Also imported was *Synod Manhatten*, a Section C stallion who was overall C and Supreme at the National Foal Show, and the same at the Ceredigion Foal Show.

KNIGHTWYND WELSH COBS
USA

Knightwynd Welsh Cobs owned by Tracy and Ruth Laufer is situated in Pennsylvania. Ruth had always had a passion for horses and ponies. As a young girl she worked at the Pittsburgh Zoo, caring for the ponies and taking the children on the pony rides. Many of the ponies used were Welsh, and so the looks and temperament of the Welsh ponies had made an indelible impression on Ruth, and when she grew up her affection for the Welsh ponies she had known was still in her heart and she was delighted to discover the Welsh Cob.

Tracy had the same love of horses but at first Ruth's passion for the Welsh drove him crazy as she was avidly researching all the material she could find on the breed, but after researching and studying the bloodlines, Tracy and Ruth began looking for a Cob.

After studying pedigrees for six years Tracy and Ruth purchased their first Welsh Cobs from Gordon Heard in 1992. These were, *Menai Mighty Model [Tyhen Comet x Menai Welsh Model]*, and *Crossroads Rose [Derwen Rebound x Derwen Railway Lady]*. *Model* had a foal at foot, *Crossroads Lady Luck [Cascob Flying Colours x Nebo Dafydd x Cascob Mary Ann]*. Both *Model* and *Rose* were covered by *Cascob Flying Colours* before leaving Crossroads Farm. The following Spring they both produced fillies and this was the start of the Knightwynds prefix, using the following sires: *Cascob Flying Colours, Parc Dilwyn, Llanarth Warwick, Hafael Brenin* and *Menai Magic's Boy*, all imported from Wales. They also leased a mare, *Okeden Honeysuckle*, and produced two fillies by *Flying Colours* out of *Honeysuckle*.

In 1997 after the death of Gordon Heard, Tracy and Ruth purchased *Cascob Flying Colours* from the estate and a friendship began between *Flyer* and Tracy as he taught Tracy the joys of driving, became his trail-riding buddy, and is now his best equine friend.

Knightwynd Welsh Cobs are used for Driving, Pony Club, and Trail Riding. Dressage will also be the future for some of the youngsters produced by the stud.

MADOC STUD
USA

Madoc Stud is owned and run by Mary Alice Williams and her daughter Miriam, who not only breed Welsh Cobs and Welsh Mountain Ponies, but also run a Riding School. Among the horses and ponies at Madoc is *Kentchurch Chime [Parc Commando x Llanarth Rhuddel]*, purchased from Anne Vestey, Kentchurch Stud, in 1983, who quickly became a favourite at the farm as he was always gentle, willing and happy to be around people. As a two year-old *Chime* was turned out with mares and the resulting foals the following spring were all that had been hoped for. Like many Cobs *Chime* developed through some gawky stages but in due course he turned into a beautiful animal with great athletic ability. He was shown under saddle in Welsh shows and later competed in pleasure driving and combined driving events when paired with first a Quarter horse and later another Cob from the Kentchurch Stud. During all this time he lived out with his mares and continued to produce exceptional foals.

In 1991 Nancy Hinz came to work at Madoc and an outstanding relationship began which resulted in the first Welsh Cob progressing to Grand Prix level in the United States. His artistic expression and flair always get high marks in the Freestyle and the crowd loves him and even cheers in the middle of the test which rather surprises some people who are used to quiet concentration in the dressage arena!

In 1997 all those associated with *Kentchurch Chime* were proud to receive his Individual Legion of Merit and are delighted at the ability and hard work of his offspring who contributed to his Sire Legion of Merit. *Chime* is one of the first Welsh to be doubly honoured and even though five offspring are needed for the award, at the end of the year six had accumulated 300 points each. *Chime*'s first foal crop produced a pair of winners, *Madoc Sarah Margaret and Trevallion Princess of Wales. Sarah* acquired her points in halter classes, under saddle and driving. The Section C *Madoc Bayberry*, out of *Madoc Bronwyn,* earned her points In-Hand and Under Saddle. Madoc Ruby, out of *Trevallion Welsh Jewel,* was also a winner In-Hand and Under Saddle. The 15.2hh *Madoc Patriot* out of *Princess Rosina* acquired his points In-Hand, Hunter and Pleasure. He is still at Madoc and has an outstanding future in the Dressage Arena.

Chime was the first Welsh Cob in the US to receive both the Legion of Merit and Sire Legion of Merit from the Welsh Pony and Cob Society of America. Also the recipient of many USDF All-Breeds Awards, he has been placed first since he was competing in fourth level and Prix St George in 1995 through Grand Prix and Grand Prix Freestyle in 1999. *Chime* has been shown in Texas, Florida, Colorado, Illinois and Maryland. Regardless of where he is showing he is always a crowd favourite. On a local level he has numerous accomplishments,

having become 1996 Intermediate 1 Regional Champion, in 1998 winning third place in the Region for Grand Prix and in 1999 the Grand Prix Freestyle Champion for the Region. *Kentchurch Chime* was retired from performance in June, 2000.

MEDWAY STUD
SOUTH AFRICA

Chris Oliver's Medway Stud is a new one and still very small. Named after the river Medway in Kent, it was started when Chris realised that the Welsh Cob stallion she had acquired to drive was actually a wonderful all-rounder and his beauty and personality were such that she fell in love with the breed. *Kallista Russell* is the Stud stallion, *Bukkenburg Ringo [Kallista Rosemary* x *Derwen Adventure Boy].* At nine years-old he has won many championships In-Hand, In-Harness and Under Saddle. As yet Chris has only two pure-bred foals by him, both of which are superb at six and seven months old and both are winners at major shows. One is *Medway Victor* who won both the General Breed foal class and the Welsh C/D class for young stock under four at the 2000 Horse of the Year, his first show.

Kallista Russell is a well-known personality at the major shows in South Africa, winning Championships In-Hand, Under Saddle and In-Harness, and he has created quite a healthy demand for these versatile ponies.

Kallista Russell [Bukkenburg x *Kallista Rosemary],* has been a consistent winner over the past two years. In 1998 at the SA Welsh Nationals he was Champion, Supreme Champion, Grand Champion, Reserve Supreme and Reserve Champion. In 1999 at the SA Welsh Nationals he was Senior Champion, Supreme Champion, Grand Champion, Reserve Supreme and Reserve Champion, amongst his long list of winnings.

Also at the stud are *Bukkenburg Gloss [Parc Crusader* x *Fronarth Gwenllian]*, an eleven year-old mare who has produced one Part-Bred foal with tremendous Dressage potential, a pure-bred filly who is currently winning in-hand and under saddle, and a colt, *Medway Victor* x *Kallista Russell*. *Gloss* has previously been SA Supreme Champion Section C/D In-Hand and also won the breed Championships at several major shows as well as the SA Champion, Private Drive. *Bukkenburg Glory [Persie Nimrod* x *Bukkenburg Grace]*, an eighteen year-old, 14hh chestnut mare, has produced very many champions, both Pure and Part-Bred. *Glory* has previously been SA Champion Section C/D In-Hand. Also at stud are *Mogambo Glenys* and *Mogambo Eliza [Derwen Rhuban Glas* x *Bukkenburg Glory]*, and lastly, *Medway Victor [Kallista Russell* x *Bukkenburg Gloss]*.

Cobs are not very plentiful in South Africa and finding suitable mares is a problem but their popularity is improving and demand certainly increasing.

MISSKARRS WELSH COBS
FINLAND

Misskarrs Stud, situated in the south-west of Finland, is owned and run by the Soderholm family.

In the beginning the stud bought their first two Welsh Cob mares from Mrs. Kirsi Lehtonen, who has imported most of the Cobs that are now in Finland. Karin Soderholm feels that thanks to Mrs Lehtonen and Mr Ifor Lloyd, Derwen, that the Stud has had a very good start with the breeding in Finland.

The first mare the stud bred from was *Stocken Lady*, by *Nebo Dafydd* x *Buckswood Isabella*, x *Derwen Regal Commander*. She was foaled in 1983. Soon after *Cwmtudu Tanwen*, by *Derwen Romeo* x *Oachatch Tegan* x *Llanarth Flying Comet*, foaled in 1984, was purchased by the stud.

Unfortunately *Stocken Lady* died in 1996 and at the time of her death she had a one month old colt foal by the stud's own stallion, *Kotimaen Regent,* at foot. This colt, named *Misskarrs Lacrimosa*, is still with them.

Cwmtudu Tanwen has produced five foals for the stud, all have proved to be excellent riding animals and now *Tanwen* herself is still there, used mostly as a riding horse.

In 1992 the stud bought a colt foal from Mrs Kirsi Lehtonen named *Kotimaen Regent*, by *Derwen Time Keeper* x *Rhystyd Rhamant* x *Derwen Replica*, who has a long list of show winnings in Finland. Before you can use a stallion at stud in Finland they have to pass an inspection for type, conformation, movement and performance. *Regent* passed his test with very high points and is an excellent riding animal and a good stock getter. He proved himself to be a prolific winner; in 1993 and 1995 he won the title of the best of all the pony breeds in Finland. In 1994 and 1995 he was Youngstock Champion and Reserve Overall Champion Welsh Cob, both times beaten by his dam, *Rhystud Rhamant*. In 1996 he was Champion Welsh Cob and also in 1997; this time he beat both his sire and dam. These shows were all judged by judges from Wales.

In 1995 *Derwen Gwawr* was purchased as a foal, by *Derwen Duke of York* x *Derwen Groten Wreiddiol*. She has so far had two foals, both by *Regent* and has been a show winner for the stud as well.

To replace *Stocken Lady* the stud bought *Derwen Days Of Old*, by *Derwen Requiem* x *Derwen Destiny*. She has now produced a filly foal by *Regent*.

In 1998 Anna Lena Yarbo from Sweden, who had been working at the same time as Karin's daughter, Lina, at Derwen, contacted Karin to say one of her *Derwen* mares was for sale. A big mare, born in 1991, *Derwen Exotic Girl* by *Derwen Quartz* x *Derwen Empress,* she joined the other *Derwen* mares. She produced a colt foal in 1999 by *Regent* and also at this time Lina purchased a two year-old filly, *Hengwm Gwen by Uplands Comet* x *Derwen Gemini*. All the mares at the stud are broken to ride.

Misskarrs Stud now has four mares, *Derwen Gwawr, Derwen Days Of Old, Derwen Exotic Girl* and *Hengwm Gwen*, also the two stallions, *Kotimaen Regent and Misskarrs Lacrimosa* and this is the stock on which the stud will base its future breeding. Karin and her family chose to breed Welsh Cobs as they consider them to be beautiful, versatile and hardy.

VLIETSTEDE
HOLLAND

Evaline de Gruyter and her partner Ruud Korst own the Vlietstede Stud. Evaline is a competitor of repute in the world of Dressage, initially competing on Dutch Warmblood horses, but during the last eight years she acquired Welsh Cobs to train instead. Ruud concentrates on driving and between them they have kept horses for many years.

They have a successful tack shop and saddlery business, both of them teach riding, and they also buy and sell Welsh Cobs, coming over to Wales frequently so that they always have Cobs in their stables for sale.

In Holland there are around fifty shows a year, all year round, indoor and outdoor, and every weekend there are Dressage, Jumping and Driving Shows throughout the country. Evaline introduced a Welsh Cob stallion to Dressage competitions and has the only one in the country competing at Medium or Advanced Medium level. This came about because she once saw Theo Pauw working with the Welsh Cob Stallion *Boshus Puzzle [Llanarth*

Gwynfor x *Nesscliffe Princess* x *Felin Prince]*, at a very high level in Dressage, so she decided that she would also like to ride a Welsh Cob.

Visiting Wales in 1998, Evaline saw several prospective horses but the one that gave her the best ride was *Abergavenny JR [Pennal Calon Lân* x *Gerrig Irene* x *Hewid Cardi]*. She liked his temperament, his bloodlines, conformation and paces and so decided to buy him. During the first two years Evaline only did some light work with him, hacking out in the fields, on the beach and on the dunes, showing him only once when he was rising four in the WPVC Spring show where he was placed second in the In-Hand class. *JR* was still growing and building up muscle, so they had to take their time before starting to really work with him. Eventually Evaline started to teach him Medium-Level Dressage movements and soon found that *Abergavenny Jr* was eager to please and very quick to learn. In the Spring of 1999 Evaline and *JR* rode in a lesson/clinic with Ellen Bontje, who was herself a member of the Dutch Olympic Team in Holland several times. *JR* was the only 'pony' in the clinic that day, but he enjoyed every minute. After the clinic she started to compete with him in Medium-Level Dressage competitions, in the same classes as the Dutch Warmblood Horses as, because of Evaline's age, she is unable to ride in a class with ponies. She found it was not always easy to compete against horses in the same class but Evaline likes his work and she has already accumulated points and also received many first prizes at this standard. *Abergavenny JR* is the youngest Cob in Holland to have ever competed at this level in dressage, possibly the only Welsh Cob stallion in Holland who is currently competing at this level.

Abergavenny JR is now the first Welsh Cob stallion in Holland noted as a 'Sport Pony', an accolade which can only be achieved when an animal has gained sufficient points in a Dressage test, or Jumping, at Advanced/Medium level. There are also only a few Welsh Part-Breds in Holland who have gained this accolade. Evaline also showed *JR* on the NWPCS Performance Day where he won the Under-Saddle class for Welsh Cobs. The judge selected the best from each Section, Welsh Mountain Pony, Section B, Section C, Section D and Welsh Part-Breds to compete for prizes in the main ring. *JR* was the only Cob to be selected to proceed to the main ring, a tough job as the entries in the Cob classes were very high. In the summer of 1999 Evaline began to ride *JR* side-saddle, and then began looking for a second Welsh Cob to do the same job, so that they could show both animals at this level, or ride a 'pas de deux', freestyle to music, side-saddle.

During the year Evaline and Ruud imported several Welsh Cobs to Holland, but none of them were big enough, or quiet enough, or did not have the right movement to do the same work in the future as *Abergavenny JR*. They attended the autumn sale of Registered Welsh Cobs in Builth Wells and Evaline spotted a gelding ten minutes before he was due to go into the sale ring. She rode him and the ride he gave her was so very good that she thought she could work with him. She then rushed to the sale ring. This horse was what she was looking for: a good temperament, a big Cob, with good conformation, plenty of bone, a good straight movement and a correct way of using his hindlegs. *Parcllwyd y Dewin [Nebo Magic* x *Parcllwyd Pride* x *Derwen Dai]*, back home in Holland, is proving to be a wonderful character; he is quick to learn and has the will to please, exactly like *JR*. Evaline and Ruud hope that he will be as good an ambassador for Welsh Cobs in Holland as his stablemate, *Abergavenny JR*.

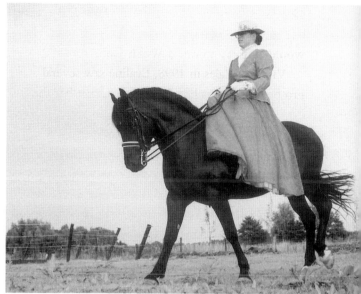

Abergavenny JR: rider and owner, Evaline de Gruyter, Holland

TO BE BORN WELSH
IS TO BE BORN PRIVILEGED

There is no doubt that the way forward for our Welsh Breeds is in performance. They are unique, and without doubt, among the best breeds in the world and, as such, they should be nurtured and preserved for generations to come.

For newcomers to the Welsh Breeds information on the Sections and the Studs in the United Kingdom can be obtained from the Welsh Pony and Cob Society who produce a yearly Journal which is free to members and can be purchased by non-members.

Other countries also have their own Welsh Pony and Cob Societies which are listed on the following page together with a selection of urls of sites of interst to breeders.

Section D mare: *Maesmynach Cymro Coch*
Photo by Maesmynach stud

FOR MORE INFORMATION:

The Welsh Pony and Cob Society
6 Chalybeate Street
Abertyswyth
Ceredigion
Wales
SY23 1HS

Tel: 01970 617501
Website: www.wpcs.uk.com

Brightwells Auctioneers
The Mews, King Street, Hereford HR4 9DB
Website: www.brightwells.com

Welsh Pony and Cob enthusiasts site:
www.welshponyandcob.co.uk

Welsh Pony and Cob Society of America:
www.welshpony.org

Welsh Pony and Cob Society of Canada:
www.welshponyandcob.org

Welsh Pony and Cob Society of Denmark:
www.welshponyer.dk

Welsh Pony and Cob Society of Holland:
www.welshpony.com

Welsh Cobs Online:
www.welshcobs-online.de

INDEX

For a full list of our publications both in
English and Welsh, ask for your free copy of our
full-colour, 40-page Catalogue.
Alternatively, surf into our website at:
www.ylolfa.com
with our NEW online shop

Y Lolfa Cyf., Talybont, Ceredigion SY24 5AP
e-mail ylolfa@ylolfa.com
internet www.ylolfa.com
phone +44 (0)1970 832 304
fax 832 782
isdn 832 813